Returning to Quarters

A History of Boston Firehouses

Richard Connelly

Order this book online at www.trafford.com/08-0757
or email orders@trafford.com

Most Trafford titles are also available at major online book retailers.

Note for Librarians: A cataloguing record for this book is available from Library
and Archives Canada at www.collectionscanada.ca/amicus/index-e.html

ISBN: 978-1-4251-8068-3 (soft)
ISBN: 978-1-4251-8069-0 (ebook)

*We at Trafford believe that it is the responsibility of us all, as both individuals
and corporations, to make choices that are environmentally and socially sound.
You, in turn, are supporting this responsible conduct each time you purchase a
Trafford book, or make use of our publishing services. To find out how you are
helping, please visit www.trafford.com/responsiblepublishing.html*

*Our mission is to efficiently provide the world's finest, most comprehensive
book publishing service, enabling every author to experience success.
To find out how to publish your book, your way, and have it available
worldwide, visit us online at www.trafford.com/10510*

 www.trafford.com

North America & international
toll-free: 1 888 232 4444 (USA & Canada)
phone: 250 383 6864 ♦ fax: 250 383 6804 ♦ email: info@trafford.com

The United Kingdom & Europe
phone: +44 (0)1865 487 395 ♦ local rate: 0845 230 9601
facsimile: +44 (0)1865 481 507 ♦ email: info.uk@trafford.com

10 9 8 7 6 5 4 3 2 1

Table of Contents

FOREWORD

This book was written over a period of approximately ten years. Photos were collected from various sources as well as my own photos of present day firehouses and buildings and locations where firehouses were formerly located. I want to thank the following for allowing me to use some photos and information from their collections:

Bill Noonan, Photographer, Boston FD
Ed Morrissey, Captain, Cambridge FD
Sid Towle's collection of BFD photos
Frank Fitzgerald, Chief, Malden FD (retired)

Without their help, this collection would have never happened. It has been a labor of love since I have always been interested in the characteristics and architecture of firehouses all over the USA.

The book starts with the downtown area and continues through the city into the annexed areas of South Boston, East Boston, Roxbury, Charlestown, Dorchester, Brighton, West Roxbury and Hyde Park.

As you pass from page to page and from chapter to chapter you will notice that I have tried to follow the history of a company from its organization until the present. Rather than go from the oldest to the newest I have tried to follow the companies in their numerical order as best as possible. For instance, in the first chapter we start with Engine 3 and follow its movement from start to finish. Then we go to Engine 4. Notice that you will not see Engine 1 until you get to the chapter on South Boston.

I have attempted to include at least one photo of each firehouse and, if possible, a historic photo and a modern day photo regardless of whether the firehouse is in service or not.

Occasionally, you will see a company number in parenthesis (E53) this means that the company has been moved to the company quarters in parenthesis.

A portion of the proceeds from the sale of this book is being donated to the Boston Firefighters Burn Foundation. This newly organized group is dedicated to helping burn victims of both firefighter families and burn victims in general. They recognize the hard work and dedication of burn unit nurses and doctors in several local hospitals including the Shriners' Burn Foundation Hospital, the Massachusetts General Hospital and others. If you would like to make a personal donation to this worthwhile cause, please go to www.bostonfirefightersburnfoundation.com.

There are numerous people whose knowledge and information contributed to my work, especially Bill Werner. Bill left us many years ago, but he left behind his thoughts and information so that others may remember how the Boston Fire Department came to be. Bill wrote the History of the Boston Fire Department, volumes one and two.

I certainly would be remiss if I didn't thank my wonderful and patient wife Julie and my daughter Hannah for putting up with my countless hours on the computer working on this book.

I sincerely hope that you, the reader, enjoy this information as much as I have enjoyed collecting it over the years.

One last word, remember to shoot that photo today because the building may be gone tomorrow.

Rick Connelly
December 2008

ABOUT THE AUTHOR

Richard 'Rick' Connelly is a Fire Captain in the Boston Fire Department. He was appointed on December 24, 1969 and assigned to Engine Company 29 in Brighton.

In 1971, he transferred to Ladder Company 20 in Roxbury/South Boston. When Ladder 20 was disbanded on February 4, 1981 he was transferred to Ladder Company 7 in Dorchester.

On March 4, 1987, he was promoted to Fire Lieutenant and served on Engine Company 10, Downtown Boston until 1988 and then transferred to Rescue Company One, Downtown Boston.

On April 10, 2007, he was promoted to Fire Captain and has again been assigned to Engine Company 10, Downtown.

Rick is married to the former Julie Ann Walrath. He has four daughters Stacey, Amy, Pamela, Hannah and a son, Rick Jr. who is a firefighter/paramedic with the Hingham, MA Fire Department.

ABOUT THE CITY OF BOSTON

The City of Boston was founded on September 17, 1630. Originally, the city was about one quarter the size that it is today. Through a series of annexations a number of surrounding towns became part of the city in a few years time.

The city of Boston's fire department was the first paid fire department in the country. It was organized in 1678 and in 1978 we celebrated the three hundredth anniversary.

In 1804 South Boston, originally called Dorchester Neck, was the first town to be annexed to the city.

East Boston became part of Boston when it was annexed in 1836.

On January 6, 1868 the town of Roxbury was annexed bringing its fire department into the City of Boston. This increased the size of the city tremendously.

Next, the town of Dorchester became part of the City of Boston. This occurred on January 3, 1870, once again nearly doubling the size of the existing city.

The next towns to be annexed to Boston were Charlestown, Brighton (Allston) and West Roxbury (Jamaica Plain and Roslindale) all on January 5, 1874.

Each of these subsequent mergers brought many more firehouses and fire companies into the city.

The final town to become part of the city was Hyde Park. This brought the City of Boston to the size that it is today. This final merger didn't take place until January 1, 1912.

There is so much history in the city that it seems like every time you turn a corner there is another historical milestone in front of you. Take a walk along the Freedom Trail. You can visit 16 historical sites, many of which you may have heard of from your history books in grade school.

Starting at the Boston Common where cows once grazed, the militia once trained and many famous orators have spoken to the citizens, you can enjoy the oldest park in America.

Continue up Beacon Hill to the golden-domed State House. This magnificent stone edifice has been expanded twice over the years.

The Park Street church with its 217 foot steeple, at the corner of Tremont and Park Streets, was the site of the first Sunday school in 1818.

The Granary Burial Ground next door to the Park Street Church is the final resting place of John Hancock, Paul Revere, Peter Faneuil, Samuel Adams, and Ben Franklin's parents. The five victims of the Boston Massacre are buried here.

Kings Chapel and Burying Ground at the corner of School and Tremont Streets is the next stop on the Freedom Trail. It was built so that the Church of England would forever have a presence in America.

The Benjamin Franklin statue on School Street, outside of the Old City Hall, overlooks the site of the first public school in America, Boston Latin School. Today Boston Latin School is situated in the Fenway section of the city.

Continue down School Street to the corner of Washington Street and you will find a plaque identifying the building on the corner as the site of the Old Corner Bookstore. It is one of the oldest original buildings in the city.

Diagonally across the street from the Old Corner Bookstore you will find the Old South Meeting House built in 1729. Here, the Boston Tea

Party had its origin when protesters of the tax on tea left the meeting house and headed for Boston Harbor where three shiploads of tea was tossed in to the harbor. This building was also saved during the Great Boston Fire in 1872. As fire neared the corner, a stand was made to save the structure and save it they did.

The Old State House on State Street is the oldest public building in the city. The Boston Massacre occurred outside the building in 1770. The Declaration of Independence was read from the balcony to the citizens of Boston in 1776.

The site of the Boston Massacre is marked by a cobblestone marker outside of the Old State House. This was the site where five colonists who were taunting the Red Coats were killed by the British soldiers in 1770.

Faneuil Hall stands at the corner of Congress and North Streets. Built in 1741, it was a market place and meeting place for many years. Today the area is a famous tourist attraction including the Quincy Market, Faneuil Hall and Samuel Adams statue.

The Paul Revere house on North Square off of North Street is one a few surviving wood frame buildings in Boston's North End. Paul Revere is most well known as both a silversmith and the rider who alerted the citizenry that "the British are coming, the British are coming".

The Old North Church on Salem Street, built in 1723, was the site of the lantern hanging, ("One if by land, two if by sea"), signaling the arrival of the British Troops on April 18, 1775. It is the oldest church building in the city.

Copp's Hill Burial Ground sits on the hill between Charter and Commercial Streets. Many famous patriots are buried at this graveyard as well as the other burial sites previously mentioned.

In the Charlestown Navy Yard sits the U.S.S. Constitution. It is the oldest commissioned warship in the U.S. Navy. It has been in the water since 1797. The former Charlestown Navy Yard was an extremely busy port for almost 175 years. One of the many ships built or repaired here is the U.S.S. Cassin Young. The Young is also on display at a dock neighboring the Constitution.

Bunker Hill Monument sits atop Breeds Hill, rising 221 feet. Climb, if you dare, the 294 steps leading to the miniscule windows at the top of this massive granite structure for a spectacular view.

Boston is home to a litany of famous Americans, most notably:

John Adams (President)
Samuel Adams (Patriot)
Louisa May Alcott (Novelist)
Crispus Attacks (Martyr of the American Revolution)
Charles Bulfinch (Architect)
James Michael Curley (Mayor)
Richard Cardinal Cushing (Cardinal of the Boston Archdiocese)
Mary Baker Eddy (Founder of the Christian Science Church)
Peter Faneuil (Philanthropist)
Arthur Fiedler (Conductor)
Benjamin Franklin (Inventor and Statesman)
John F. Fitzgerald (Honey Fitz)
William Lloyd Garrison (Abolishionist)
Cotton Mather (Clergyman)
John W. McCormack (Speaker of the House)
Samuel Morse (Morse Code)
Edgar Allen Poe (Author)
Paul Revere (Silversmith and Messenger of the Revolution)
Thomas P. "Tip" O'Neill (Speaker of the House)

Some of the most famous historical incidents which occurred here are:

The Boston Massacre (March 5, 1770)
The Boston Tea Party (December 16, 1773)
The Battle of Bunker Hill (June 17, 1775)
The Great Boston Fire (November 9, 1872)
The Molasses Flood (January 15, 1919)
Boston Police Strike (September 19, 1919)
Luongo Restaurant Fire – Six Firefighters killed (November 15, 1942)
Cocoanut Grove Fire – 492 lives lost (November 28, 1942)
Trumbull Street Fire – Five Firefighters killed (October 1, 1964)
The Vendome Hotel Fire – Nine Firefighters killed (June 17, 1972)

Boston's Famed Institutions:

America's first subway system
Boston Latin School, April 23, 1635 (America's first public school)
Bunker Hill Monument
Faneuil Hall
Fenway Park
Old North Church
Quincy Market
U.S.S. Constitution (U. S. Navy's oldest commissioned warship, 1797)

Boston's Hospitals:

Beth Israel Deaconess Medical Center
Boston Medical Center
Boston University Medical Center
Brigham and Women's Hospital
Carney Hospital
Children's Hospital, Boston
Dana Farber Cancer Institute
Faulkner Hospital
Franciscan Childrens' Hospital
Harvard Medical School
Harvard School of Public Health
Harvard School of Dental Medicine
Jewish Memorial Hospital
Lemuel Shattuck Hospital
Mass Eye and Ear Infirmary
Massachusetts General Hospital
New England Baptist Hospital
New England Medical Center
St. Elizabeth's Hospital
Shriners' Burns Institute
Spaulding Rehabilitation Hospital
Tufts Dental School
Tufts Medical Center
Tufts University School of Medicine
Veterans Administration Hospital, Jamaica Plain
Veterans Administration Hospital, West Roxbury

Boston's Schools and Colleges:

Berklee School of Music
Boston College (portions)
Boston Conservatory
Boston University
Bunker Hill Community College
Emerson College
Emmanuel College
Harvard School of Law
Harvard School of Medicine
Mass College of Art
Mass College of Pharmacy
New England Conservatory of Music
New England School of Law
Northeastern University
Roxbury Community College
Simmons College
Suffolk University
Tufts Dental School
Tufts Medical Center
University of Massachusetts, Boston
Wentworth Institute of Technology
Wheelock College

FIREHOUSE LOCATION CHART - 2008

DIVISION ONE (E10)				
District	**Engine**	**Ladder**	**Special**	**Address**
District 1 (E5)	Engine 5			360 Saratoga Street, East Boston
	Engine 9	Ladder 2		239 Sumner Street, East Boston
	Engine 56	Ladder 21		1 Ashley Street, East Boston
District 3 (E4)	Engine 4	Ladder 24		200 Cambridge Street, Boston
	Engine 8	Ladder 1		392 Hanover Street, Boston
	Engine 50			34 Winthrop Street, Charlestown
	Marine Unit			Burroughs Wharf, Boston
District 4 (E7)	Engine 3		Special Unit (H2)	618 Harrison Avenue, Boston
	Engine 7	Tower Ladder 17		200 Columbus Avenue, Boston
	Engine 22	Haz-Mat Unit (H3)	Rehab Unit (W25)	700 Tremont Street
	Engine 33	Ladder 15		941 Boylston Street, Boston
District 6 (E39)	Engine 2	Ladder 19		700 East Fourth Street, South Boston
	Engine 10	Tower Ladder 3	Rescue 1 & Collapse Unit	125 Purchase Street, Boston
	Engine 39	Ladder 18	Decon Unit	272 D Street, South Boston
District 11 (E29)	Engine 29	Ladder 11		138 Chestnut Hill Avenue, Brighton
	Engine 41	Ladder 14		460 Cambridge Street, Allston
	Engine 51			425 Faneuil Street, Brighton

DIVISION TWO (E28)				
District 5 (E37)	Engine 14	Ladder 4	Safety Division (H1)	174 Dudley Street, Roxbury
	Engine 37	Ladder 26		560 Huntiington Avenue, Roxbury
District 7 (E17)	Engine 17	Ladder 7		7 Parish Street, Dorchester
	Engine 21			641 Columbia Road, Dorchester
	Engine 24	Ladder 23		36 Washington Street, Dorchester
District 8 (E16)	Engine 16			9 Gallivan Boulevard, Dorchester
	Engine 18	Ladder 6		1884 Dorchester Avenue, Dorchester
	Engine 20			301 Neponset Avenue, Dorchester
	Fire Brigade			Long Island, Boston Harbor
District 9 (E42)	Engine 28	Tower Ladder 10		746 Centre Street, Jamaica Plain
	Engine 42		Rescue 2	1870 Columbus Avenue, Roxbury
District 10 (E55)	Engine 30	Ladder 25		1940 Centre Street, West Roxbury
	Engine 49			209 Neponset Valley Pkwy, Readville
	Engine 55		Brush Unit 55	5115 Washington Street, West Roxbury
District 12 (E53)	Engine 48	Ladder 28	Brush Unit 48	60 Fairmount Avenue, Hyde Park
	Engine 52	Ladder 29		975 Blue Hill Avenue, Dorchester
	Engine 53	Ladder 16		945 Canterbury Street, Roslindale

1

Boston Proper

Some of you may recognize this as the name of a television show. This term was always used to describe the original area of Boston. Beacon Hill, Downtown and the North and South End sections are included. Today (2009) Districts 3 and 4 cover this area.

The Boston Proper section of the book has the most pages and the most firehouses for a couple of reasons. First, it is the oldest section of the city and secondly, because of the gargantuan renovation of the downtown area, firehouses have moved, been razed, and have had companies join other companies over the years.

The downtown area is the main office area, the financial district, the shopping district and home to many fine restaurants and historic tourist attractions. The North End is a tenement district, one traditionally occupied by Italian families. Today, there is a much larger transient type of population in the North End. It is still Boston's answer to the Little Italy section of New York City. Street after street, and block after block of fine foods served in large restaurants or tiny bistros that have become so well known in Boston. When tourists ask which restaurants are good, my reply is usually, "If they're not good, they don't stay in business around here."

The South End is also a tenement district; however, these residences were at one time brownstone one-family walkups. Over the years, most have been converted to multi-family buildings. In the 60s and 70s, the South End became run down and invited a somewhat questionable element. Nighttime on the streets was daring. In the late 80s, 90s and into the 2000s, this area has made a major rebound. The area has become, as they say, "Gentrified". Real Estate has become practically untouchable. These buildings are over one hundred years old and are absolutely beautiful. Most have a steep flight of stairs for entry to the main floor with another door under the stairs leading to the lower level. This section of Boston is also home to many hospitals, schools, hotels, and trendy businesses.

In the Back Bay, you will find many extravagant hotels and restaurants, most offering outdoor seating. The wealthy Newbury Street area is famed for its unique shops, art galleries and personal grooming businesses.

Beacon Hill's most famous building is the golden domed State House. Elaborate in appearance as it overlooks the Boston Common, once a grazing area for the cows and sheep of the residents in the 1600s and 1700s. If you meander through the streets of Beacon Hill, take notice of the elaborate doorways and the different door knockers adorning these doors.

Next door to the Boston Common is the Public Garden, which is just that. A public garden area festooned with blooming flowers of every kind in the spring and summer. It has been here in its glory since 1837 when it became the first public botanical garden in the United States. It is also home to the world's smallest suspension bridge which was constructed in 1867. It is where you will find the famous swan boats. These boats are fashioned to look like a swan pushing one half dozen rows of benches where you may take a leisurely glide around the pond. These boats are powered by the pedaling of the 'captain' of the ship. Every spring Romeo and Juliet are brought back to roam the pond. They are two majestic swans that have graced the Public Garden for years. By the way, the swan boats have been run by the Paget family for almost 150 years.

Swan boat in the Public Garden
(Courtesy of the 'Swan Boats of Boston')

1171 WASHINGTON STREET south of DOVER STREET

Built: Prior to December 1, 1859

Closed: August 19, 1901 – Building razed

Occupied by Hand Engine 3 until the organization of Engine 3 on December 1, 1859.

Occupied by Engine 3 from date of organization on December 1, 1859 until April 1, 1875 when the company moved to a new firehouse at 440 Harrison Avenue.

Occupied by Aerial Ladder 1 from an indefinite date in 1880 until June 30, 1883 when it was moved back to Fort Hill Square. (E25)

Occupied by Ladder Company 13 from date of organization on June 30, 1883 until August 19, 1901 when Ladder 13 moved to 70 Warren Avenue (E22).

Horse drawn Ladder 13 at 1171 Washington Street, South End

HARRISON AVENUE & EAST BROOKLINE STREET

Built: 1850

Closed: 1862 – Building razed, site occupied today by a public housing project.

Occupied by Ladder 3 until 1862 when they moved to new quarters at Harrison Avenue and Wareham Street. (E3)

11 WAREHAM STREET (Fire Alarm Shop)

Built: 1862

Closed: unknown – Building razed

Occupied by the Lighting Plant from November 23, 1925 until September 25, 1928 when a new Lighting Plant was placed in service at 60 Bristol Street.

Occupied by the Lighting Plant from May 4, 1929 until December 16, 1947 when its designation was changed to Lighting Plant 1.

Occupied by Lighting Plant 1 from December 16, 1947 until May 1, 1956 when all Lighting Plants were placed in reserve.

HARRISON AVENUE & WAREHAM STREET

Built: 1862

Closed: 1875 – This house was converted into a repair shop after the companies relocated.

Building was later razed and is a park today.

Occupied by Ladder 3 from 1862 until they moved to a new firehouse at 440 Harrison Avenue on April 1, 1875.

Occupied by Extinguisher Wagon No. 2 from date of organization on April 1, 1872 until April 27, 1874 when they were disbanded.

Firehouse on Harrison Avenue which housed Engine 3 and Ladder 3

440 HARRISON AVENUE, corner of BRISTOL STREET.

Built: April 1, 1875

Closed: December 8, 1937 – Building razed

Occupied by Engine 3 from April 1, 1875 until December 8, 1937 when the company moved to temporary quarters at 60 Bristol Street.

Occupied by Ladder 3 from April 1, 1875 until December 8, 1937 when the company moved to temporary quarters at 60 Bristol Street.

Firehouse at 444 Harrison Avenue

60 BRISTOL STREET

Built: January 11, 1894

Closed: August 6, 1951 – Still standing and currently used as private building.

Occupied by Water Tower 2 from date of organization on December 18, 1893 until April 17, 1928 when Water Tower 2 was relocated to a new firehouse at 194 Broadway. (L17)

Occupied by Foamite Unit 1 from date of organization on November 9, 1925 until November 26, 1926 when Foamite Unit 1 was relocated to 198 Dudley Street. (L4)

Occupied by Water Tower 2 again from January 23, 1946 until June 26, 1950 when it was again relocated to 194 Broadway. (L17)

Occupied by Engine 3 temporarily from December 8, 1937 until they moved to a new firehouse at 618 Harrison Avenue on April 28, 1941.

Occupied by Ladder 3 temporarily from December 8, 1937 until they moved to a new firehouse at 618 Harrison Avenue on April 28, 1941.

Occupied temporarily by Engine 22 from May 9, 1899 until August 1, 1901 while a new firehouse was being constructed at 70 Warren Avenue.

Occupied by Lighting Plant from September 25, 1928 until May 4, 1929 when a new Lighting Plant was in service at the Fire Alarm Shop at 11 Wareham Street.

60 Bristol Street with the drill tower in the rear

Richard Connelly

618 HARRISON AVENUE

Built: April 28, 1941

Still in service

Occupied by Engine 3 from April 28, 1941 until present.

Occupied by Ladder 3 from April 28, 1941 until March 23, 1970 when Ladder 3 was disbanded and reorganized as Aerial Tower 1.

Occupied by Aerial Tower 1 from March 23, 1970 until April 10, 1981 when the company was deactivated.

Occupied by Lighting Plant 2 from January 21, 1948 until August 20, 1951 when it was moved to 900 Massachusetts Avenue. (E23)

Occupied by Lighting Plant 2 again from July 13, 1954 until May 1, 1956 when all Lighting Plants were placed in reserve.

Occupied by the Special Unit (formerly Lighting Plant 1) from the date of organization on July 27, 1987 until present.

Engine 3 and Ladder 3 in the 1950s

Engine 3 and the Special Unit's firehouse today

CITY HALL, COURT SQUARE

No dates available – Building razed

Occupied by Hand Engine 11 before being occupied by Steam Engine 4, which was organized on May 7, 1860 in the basement of City Hall.

Occupied by Engine 4 from May 7, 1860 until sometime in 1862 when the company moved to Scollay's Building in Scollay Square near Court Street and Cornhill.

SCOLLAY'S BUILDING at SCOLLAY SQ. near. COURT ST. and CORNHILL

No dates available – Building razed

Occupied by Engine 4 from sometime in 1862 until an unknown date in December 1870 when the company moved to Smith's stable on Bulfinch Street.

SMITH'S STABLE ON BULFINCH STREET

No dates available – Building razed

Occupied by Engine 4 from an indefinite date in December 1870 until December 12, 1872 when the new firehouse at 5 Bulfinch Street was opened and the company was relocated.

5 BULFINCH STREET, WEST END

Built: December 12, 1872

Closed: February 25, 1929 – Building razed, area today is occupied by government properties.

Note: First sliding pole in Boston installed here in 1880.

Note: Engine 4 was the first fire company to have rubber tires.

Occupied by Engine 4 from December 12, 1872 until February 25, 1929 when Engine 4 moved to a temporary location with Ladder 24 at 16 North Grove Street.

Occupied by Extinguisher Wagon No. 1 from December 12, 1872 until February 9, 1873 when Extinguisher Wagon No. 1 was disbanded and Chemical Engine 1 was organized.

Occupied by Chemical Engine 1 from date of organization on February 9, 1873 until the company was disbanded on September 16, 1921.

Occupied by Water Tower from June 30, 1883 until December 18, 1893 when it became designated Water Tower 1.

Occupied by Ladder 1 from December 12, 1893 until January 1895 when the company moved into a new firehouse at 152 Friend Street.

Occupied by Water Tower 1 from December 18, 1893 until September 14, 1923 when it was relocated to Fort Hill Square. (E25)

Occupied temporarily by Engine 26 from October 9, 1925 until April 17, 1928 when the company moved to a new fire station at 194 Broadway. (L17)

Occupied temporarily by the pumper of Engine 35 from October 9, 1925 until April 17, 1928 when Engine 35 was relocated to a new firehouse at 194 Broadway.

Bulfinch Street firehouse

MERRIMAC STREET

Very little information available about this location.

Occupied by Ladder 1 from date of organization on August 4, 1820 until March 14, 1853 when Ladder 1 was relocated to an old school on Friend Street

FRIEND STREET, SCHOOLHOUSE

Once again very little information is known about this building

Occupied by Ladder 1 from March 14, 1853 until December 12, 1893 when the company was moved to 5 Bulfinch Street. (E4)

152 FRIEND STREET (WARREN SQUARE)

Built: January 1895

Closed: October 17, 1933 – Building razed

Occupied by Ladder 1 from January 1895 until October 17, 1933 when the company moved to Bowdoin Square (E4) and the Friend Street firehouse was abandoned.

Ladder 1's former quarters on Friend Street

BOWDOIN SQUARE

Built: November 10, 1930

Closed: October 28, 1963 – Building razed for Government Center construction

Occupied by Engine 4 from November 10, 1930 until October 28, 1963 when the company was temporarily relocated to 123 Oliver Street. (E25)

Occupied by Ladder 24 from November 10, 1930 until October 28, 1963 when the company was temporarily relocated to 123 Oliver Street. (E25)

Occupied by Water Tower 1 from November 14, 1930 until October 17, 1933 when it was relocated to Fort Hill Square.

Occupied by Rescue 3 from November 14, 1930 until January 1, 1955 when the company would now be known as the Rescue Company.

Occupied by Ladder 1 from October 17, 1933 until September 22, 1948 when they moved to 392 Hanover Street. (E8)

Again occupied by Water Tower 1 from December 16, 1943 until May 1, 1956 when its assignments were canceled and Water Tower 1 was placed in reserve.

Occupied temporarily by Engine 10 from February 15, 1946 until April 14, 1949 while a new firehouse was being constructed for Engine 10 on the site of their old quarters at Mt. Vernon and River Streets. (127 Mt. Vernon Street)

Occupied by the new Lighting Plant 3 from November 4, 1947 until January 21, 1948 when Lighting Plant 13 was relocated to 36 Washington Street in Dorchester. (L23)

Occupied by Lighting Plant 1 from January 21, 1948 until May 1, 1956 when all Lighting Plants were placed in reserve.

Occupied by Engine 6 from date of reactivation on April 27, 1949 until Engine 6 was again deactivated on July 13, 1954.

Occupied by the Rescue Company from January 1, 1955 until June 11, 1960 when the Rescue Company moved to 123 Oliver Street. (E25)

Occupied by District 4 until February 25, 1929 when they moved to temporary quarters with Engine 6 and again from November 10, 1930 until May 4, 1954 when districts were reorganized with District 4 becoming District 3.

Occupied by District 3 from May 4, 1954 until October 28, 1963 when they moved to a temporary location at 123 Oliver Street. (E25)

This was the largest firehouse in the city

200 CAMBRIDGE STREET, BEACON HILL

Built: May 3, 1965

Still in service

Occupied by Engine 4 from May 3, 1965 until present.

Occupied by Ladder 24 from May 3, 1965 until present.

Occupied by District 3 from May 3, 1965 until present.

Occupied temporarily by Ladder 1 from November 23, 1987 until March 8, 1988 while the firehouse at 392 Hanover Street had major repairs done to its floor.

This plain, nondescript building replaced the ornate Bowdoin Square firehouse

30 WALL STREET between Causeway & Cotting Streets, WEST END

Built: Prior to 1859

Closed: July 31, 1888 - Building razed, now part of Charles River Park Apartments

Occupied by Steam Engine "Eclipse" without a regular company of men assigned from January 1, 1859 until January 1, 1860. The company was to be operated by the builder of the "Eclipse."

Occupied by Hand Engine 6 from date of organization on January 1, 1860 using the "Eclipse" until May 1, 1874 when the company was reorganized to become Engine 6.

Occupied by Engine 6 from date of organization on May 1, 1874 until July 31, 1888 when the company moved to a newly built firehouse at 26 Leverett Street.

26 LEVERETT STREET, WEST END

Built: July 31, 1888

Closed: November 13, 1930

Building razed, now part of Charles River Park Apartments

Occupied by Engine 6 from July 31, 1888 until November 13, 1930 when the company moved to the newly built Bowdoin Square firehouse.

OLD QUARTERS OF ENGINE COMPANY 6, LEVERETT STREET,
REPLACED BY NEW FIRE STATION IN BOWDOIN SQUARE.

Leverett Street in the old West End

Leverett Street firehouse in its final days

FRUIT STREET, WEST END

BUILT: Prior to 1860

CLOSED: June 1, 1869 – Building razed, now Massachusetts General Hospital property.

Occupied by Horse Hose 3 from date of organization on June 16, 1860 until June 1, 1869 when the company moved to a new firehouse at 16 N. Grove Street.

16 NORTH GROVE STREET, BEACON HILL

Built: June 1, 1869

Closed: November 12, 1930 – Building razed, now part of Massachusetts General Hospital property.

Occupied by Hose 3 from June 1, 1869 until the company was renumbered as Hose 8 on May 17, 1875.

Occupied by Hose 8 from May 17, 1875 until the company was disbanded on December 20, 1895.

Occupied by Extinguisher Wagon No. 1 from date of organization on May 1, 1871 until December 21, 1872 when the company moved to a new firehouse at 5 Bulfinch Street. (E4)

Occupied by Chemical 11 from date of organization on December 20, 1895 until the company was disbanded on November 1, 1899.

Occupied by Combination Ladder 8 from date of organization on November 1, 1899 until April 21, 1905 when the company designation changed to Ladder Company 24.

Occupied by Ladder Company 24 from date of organization on April 21, 1905 until November 12, 1930 when the company moved to a new firehouse at Bowdoin Square.

Occupied by Engine 4 from February 25, 1929 until November 10, 1930 when the company moved to new firehouse at Bowdoin Sq.

This site is now a parking garage for the Massachusetts General Hospital

398 SHAWMUT AVENUE, SOUTH END

Built: March 15,1847

Closed: October 26, 1917 – building razed, now residential

Occupied by Hand Hose 5 prior to August 17, 1860 when Horse Hose 5 was organized.

Occupied by Horse Hose 5 from August 17, 1860 until the company was disbanded on December 20, 1895.

Occupied by Chemical 4 from date of organization on December 20, 1895 until the company was disbanded on October 26, 1917 and this firehouse was closed.

Chemical 4 outside the firehouse on Shawmut Avenue in the South End

HUDSON STREET, near OAK STREET, CHINATOWN

BUILT: Prior to May 1, 1860

CLOSED: May 17, 1875 – Building razed

Occupied by Hand Hose 2 sometime prior to May 1, 1860 when Hose 2 was organized.

Occupied by Hose 2 from May 1, 1860 until May 17, 1875 when the company was disbanded and this firehouse abandoned.

PURCHASE STREET near HARTFORD STREET

BUILT: Prior to 1859

CLOSED: September 25, 1870 – Building razed

Occupied by Hand Engine 7 from sometime prior to 1859 until the company was reorganized as Steam Engine "Lawrence" on January 1, 1859.

Occupied by Steam Engine "Lawrence" from January 1, 1859. The company was organized without a regular company of men. It was to be operated by builder. The company was disbanded on January 1, 1860 and reorganized as Engine 7.

Occupied by Engine 7 from date of organization on January 1, 1860 until September 25, 1870 when the company moved to a new firehouse at 7 East Street.

Purchase Street firehouse when Engine 7 was known as T. C. Amory 7

7 EAST STREET (1)

BUILT: September 25, 1870

CLOSED: August 10, 1922 – Building razed for new firehouse

Occupied by Engine 7 from September 25, 1870 until August 10, 1922 when the firehouse was razed to make way for a new firehouse on this site. The company was temporarily relocated to Fort Hill Square (E25).

7 EAST STREET (2)

BUILT: June 27, 1923

CLOSED: November 12, 1953

Still standing – Presently used as a commercial building

Occupied by Engine 7 from June 27, 1923 until November 12, 1953 when the firehouse was closed and the company moved to 123 Oliver Street. (E25)

Occupied by District 5 from October 9, 1925 until April 17, 1928 when they relocated to 194 Broadway. (E26)

Occupied again by District 5 from August 9, 1939 until September 11, 1953 when they moved to 123 Oliver Street. (E25)

This was the second firehouse on this site

7 East Street as it exists today

Richard Connelly

NORTH BENNETT STREET, NORTH END

Built: December 1, 1859

Closed: 1868

Building still standing, now residential

Occupied by Engine 8 from date of organization on November 1, 1859 until an unknown date in March 1868 when the company moved to a newly built firehouse at 133 Salem Street.

The old firehouse is private residences today

112 SALEM STREET, NORTH END

Built: Prior to April 1 1860

Closed: 1868 - Building still standing, now residential

Occupied by Hand Hose 1 prior to April 1, 1860.

Occupied by Horse Hose 1 from date of organization on April 1, 1860 until sometime in March 1868 when the company moved to a new firehouse at 133 Salem Street. (E8)

Another old firehouse converted into a restaurant and apartments above

Richard Connelly

133 SALEM STREET, NORTH END

Built: March, 1868

Closed: September 15, 1948

Presently used as a commercial building

Occupied by Engine 8 from March 1868 until October 30, 1916 when Engine 8 temporarily moved to the North End Paving Yard with the men being quartered at Engine 31's quarters at 521 Commercial Street.

Occupied by Horse Hose 1 from an indefinite date in March 1868 until the company was disbanded on October 1, 1873.

Note: Between October 18, 1916 and July 5, 1917 the firehouse on Salem Street was being remodeled.

Occupied by Engine 8 from July 5, 1917, upon completion of renovations, until September 15, 1948 when Engine 8 moved to their newly built quarters at 392 Hanover Street.

Engine 8 ran out of this firehouse at 133 Salem St.

Today Sheldon's Bargain Outlet does business here

Boston's North End is famous for its multitude of Italian restaurants, on both the main streets and tucked away on side streets and down tiny alleys. The neighborhood was traditionally Italian families living here for generation after generation. Today has seen a new type of neighbor. The North End has become a transient neighborhood with singles and young couples moving in to be close to work. The longtime residents are moving to the suburbs or, as the older generations pass on, the Italian families are gradually being phased out.

392 HANOVER STREET, NORTH END

Built: September 15, 1948

Still in service

Occupied by Engine 8 from September 15, 1948 until present.

Occupied by Ladder 1 from September 22, 1948 until present.

Occupied temporarily by Division 1 from September 26, 1952 until September 11, 1953 when they moved to the new firehouse at 123 Oliver Street. (E25)

From November 23, 1987 until March 8, 1988 Engine 8 was temporarily relocated to 123 Oliver Street (E10) and Ladder 1 was temporarily relocated to 200 Cambridge Street (L24) while the floor in their quarters was being replaced.

From April 12, 1999 until October 26, 1999 Engine 8 was temporarily relocated to Marine Unit's quarters on Burrough's Wharf while their firehouse was being renovated. Ladder 1 remained in quarters.

From June 20, 2005 until October 17, 2005 Engine 8 and Ladder 1 were temporarily located adjacent to the U. S. Coast Guard base on Commercial Street while the firehouse was again being remodeled.

Engine 8 and Ladder 1 today

MT. VERNON AND RIVER STS. (1), BEACON HILL

Built: Prior to 1860

Closed: February 14, 1946

Building razed for construction of new firehouse on same site.

Occupied by Hand Engine 4 from sometime prior to 1860 until the company was designated Horse Hose 7 on August 1, 1860.

Occupied by Horse Hose 7 from August 1, 1860 until the company was disbanded on June 1, 1862.

Occupied by Engine Company 10 from date of organization on June 1, 1862 until February 14, 1946 when the company was temporarily relocated to 194 Broadway (E26) while this firehouse was being razed and new quarters were built on the original site.

RIVER ST. - TORN DOWN 1947.
FORMER QUARTERS OF

First firehouse at this location

127 MT. VERNON STREET, BEACON HILL

Built: April 14, 1949

Closed: 1987

Still standing - currently occupied by Hill House, a community center, previously used as a set for MTV's Real World.

Occupied by Engine 10 from April 14, 1949 until January 14, 1982 when the company was relocated to 123 Oliver Street. (R1)

Occupied by Safety Division Chief (H1) from the date of organization on September 13, 1983 until an indefinite date in 1987 when they relocated to 301 Neponset Ave. (E20)

Second firehouse on this site

As the building at 127 Mt. Vernon Street sits today

FORT HILL SQUARE   (Washington Square at Belcher Lane)

BUILT: October 1, 1873

CLOSED: September 26, 1952 - Building razed for construction of highway exit ramp.

Note: In September 1875 a hose and harness shop was established in this firehouse.

Occupied by Engine 25 from date of organization on October 1, 1873 until September 26, 1952 when the company moved to a temporary location at 9 Pittsburgh Street in South Boston. (L18)

Occupied by Ladder 8 from date of organization on October 1, 1873 until September 26, 1952 when they temporarily relocated to 344 Congress Street in South Boston. (E39)

Occupied by Aerial Ladder 1 from March 28, 1876 until an indefinite date in 1880 when the ladder truck was moved to 1171 Washington Street.

Occupied by Aerial Ladder 1 again, however it was now designated as Ladder 14, from June 30, 1883 until April 23, 1915 when the company was disbanded.

Occupied by the Water Tower from date of organization on March 20, 1882 until June 30, 1883 when it was relocated to 5 Bulfinch St. (E4)

Occupied by Rescue 1 from date of organization on June 15, 1917 until June 5, 1922 when Rescue 1 relocated to 25 Church Street.

Occupied by Water Tower 1 from September 14, 1923 until November 14, 1930 when it was relocated to Bowdoin Square. (E4)

Occupied again by Water Tower 1 from October 17, 1933 until December 16, 1943 when it was again relocated to Bowdoin Square. (E4)

Occupied by Engine 7 temporarily from August 10, 1922 until June 27, 1923 when the company moved to a new firehouse at 7 East Street.

Occupied by Engine 7 temporarily during 1937 while their quarters on East Street were being remodeled.

Occupied by District 3 from August1, 1912 until June 9, 1909 when they were relocated to 9 Pittsburgh Street. (L18)

Occupied by Division 1 from June 9, 1909 until February 4, 1947 when they relocated to 70 Warren Avenue. (E22) There was now to be only one deputy chief on duty.

Occupied by Division 1 from January 19, 1949 until September 26, 1952 when they were temporarily relocated to E8's quarters at 392 Hanover Street.

The Fort Hill Square firehouse

Another view of Fort Hill Square

123 OLIVER STREET

BUILT: September 11, 1953

CLOSED: August 30, 1989 - Building razed for construction of office tower.

Occupied by Engine 25 from September 11, 1953 until February 4, 1981 when the company was deactivated due to Proposition 2 ½.

Occupied by Ladder 8 from September 11, 1953 until April 10, 1981 when the company was deactivated due to Proposition 2 ½.

Occupied by Water Tower 2 from July 13, 1954 until May 1, 1956 when its assignments were canceled and it was placed in reserve.

Occupied by the Rescue Company from June 11, 1960 until October 25, 1972 when the company was designated as Rescue 1.

Occupied by Rescue 1 from October 25, 1972 until August 30, 1989 when they moved into a new firehouse at 125 Purchase Street.

Occupied by Lighting Plant 1 when it was again placed in service on May 3, 1967 until May 11, 1971 when Special Unit 1 and Lighting Plant 1 were combined as one.

Occupied by Special Unit 1 from February 19, 1969 until May 11, 1971 when Special Unit 1 and Lighting Plant 1 were combined as one

Occupied by Division 1 from September 11, 1953 until August 30, 1989 when they moved into a new firehouse at 125 Purchase Street.

Occupied by Engine 7 from November 12, 1953 until July 13, 1954 when the company moved to 194 Broadway. (E26)

Occupied by District 5 from September 11, 1953 until March 31, 1954 when district headquarters was moved to 194 Broadway. (E26)

Occupied by Engine 4 temporarily from October 28, 1963 until May 3, 1965 when the new firehouse opened at 200 Cambridge Street.

Occupied by Ladder 24 temporarily from October 28, 1963 until May 3, 1965 when the new firehouse opened at 200 Cambridge Street.

Occupied temporarily by District 3 from October 28, 1963 until May 3, 1965 when they moved to the new firehouse at 200 Cambridge Street. (E4)
Occupied by Engine 10 from January 14, 1982 until August 30, 1989 when they moved into a new firehouse at 125 Purchase Street.

Occupied by Tower Company from date of organization on May 21, 1983 until August 30, 1989 when they moved into a new firehouse at 125 Purchase Street.

Occupied by the Haz-Mat Company from the date of organization on May 1, 1985 until August 30, 1989 when they moved into a new firehouse at 125 Purchase Street.

Occupied by Engine 8 from November 23, 1987 until March 8, 1988 while the firehouse at 392 Hanover Street had major repairs done to its floor.

The building behind this firehouse was imploded in 1988 to make way for the construction of new office towers that would include a firehouse to replace this one. The firehouse was also razed after completion of the new building.

125 PURCHASE STREET

BUILT: August 30, 1989

Still in service. Firehouse is in the first two floors of an office tower.

Occupied by Engine 10 from August 30, 1989 until present.

Occupied by Tower Company from August 30, 1989 until September 7, 2002 when the company was designated Tower Ladder 3.

Occupied by Tower Ladder 3 from September 7, 2002 until present.

Occupied by Rescue 1 from August 30, 1989 until present.

Occupied by Division 1 from August 30, 1989 until present.

Occupied by Haz-Mat (H3) from August 30, 1989 until July 1, 1997 when it was relocated to 945 Canterbury Street (E53)

125 Purchase Street

WARREN STREET (Now known as WARRENTON ST.), PARK SQUARE

Built: Prior to 1860

Closed: April 1, 1869 - Building since razed

Occupied by Hand Engine 12 from sometime prior to 1860 until the company was reorganized as Horse Hose 8 on July 1, 1860.

Occupied by Horse Hose 8 from date of organization on July 1, 1860 until April 1, 1869 when Hose 8 moved to a new firehouse at 25 Church Street.

PARKER STREET (Now known as HEMENWAY ST.), BACK BAY

Built: October 14, 1873

Closed: July 3, 1875 - Building razed

Engine 22 was organized on October 14, 1873 and quartered in a wooden building in an undetermined location on Parker Street near Boylston Street until August 1875 when they moved to a new firehouse on Dartmouth Street.

DARTMOUTH STREET opposite BUCKINGHAM STREET, BACK BAY

Built: June 26, 1875

Closed: May 9, 1899 - Building razed, now the site of Copley Place Mall

Occupied by Engine 22 from June 26, 1875 until May 9, 1899 when the firehouse was closed and razed for construction of a railroad station. Engine Company 22 was temporarily relocated to 60 Bristol Street. (E3)

The Dartmouth Street firehouse. The beautiful Back Bay railroad station was built on this site. In return for the property, the railroad built the new firehouse at 70 Warren Avenue to replace the old firehouse on Dartmouth Street.

70 WARREN AVENUE, SOUTH END

Built: August 1, 1901 – Built by the New York, New Haven and Hartford Railroad.

Closed: June 11, 1960 – Currently used as: Private residences

Occupied by Engine 22 from August 1, 1901 until June 11, 1960 when the company moved to a new firehouse at 700 Tremont Street.

Occupied by Ladder 13 from August 19, 1901 until June 11, 1960 when they moved to a new firehouse at 700 Tremont Street.

Occupied by District 7 from August 19, 1901 until May 4, 1954 when District 7 became District 4.

Occupied by District 4 from May 4, 1954 until June 11, 1960 when they moved to a new firehouse at 700 Tremont Street. (E22)

Occupied by Division 2 upon the reestablishment of three divisions on September 14, 1913 until the abolishment of Division 3 on March 14, 1914 and the relocation of Division 2 to 198 Dudley Street. (L4)

Again occupied by Division 2 upon departmental reorganization into three divisions on July 5, 1919.

Occupied temporarily by Engine 23 from March 28, 1948 until they moved again on May 16, 1949 to 198 Dudley Street. (L4)

On January 5, 1949 the department again reduced to two divisions with Division 1 remaining at 70 Warren Avenue until January 19, 1949.

On January 19, 1949 the department was again reorganized into three divisions. The existing Division 1 was renumbered as Division 2 and remained at 70 Warren Avenue. The new Division 1 was located at Fort Hill Square (L8) and Division 3 again located at 36 Washington Street. (L23)

70 Warren Avenue in its heyday

And today as residences....

700 TREMONT STREET, SOUTH END

Built: June 11, 1960

Still in service

Occupied by Engine 22 from June 11, 1960 until present.

Occupied by Ladder 13 from June 11, 1960 until October 20, 1981 when the company was deactivated during Proposition 2 ½.

Occupied by District 4 from June 11, 1960 until May 10, 1971 when the district headquarters was relocated to a new firehouse at 200 Columbus Avenue. (E7)

Temporarily occupied by Ladder 26 from June 1, 1995 until November 6, 1995 while the firehouse at 560 Huntington Avenue was being remodeled.

Occupied by Rehab unit (G-25) from 1996 until present.

Occupied by Haz-Mat Unit (H3) from November 1, 2001 until present.

One of only a few one story firehouses in the city

157 HARRISON AVENUE, CHINATOWN

BUILT: May 18, 1891

CLOSED: January 7, 1946

Building razed, now part of Tufts New England Medical Center

Occupied by Ladder 17 from the date of their organization on May 18, 1891 until November 9, 1925 when they relocated to a temporary location at 7 Whitmore Street while their quarters were being remodeled.

Occupied by Ladder 17 from February 17, 1926 until January 7, 1946 when the company was relocated to 194 Broadway (E26) and this firehouse was abandoned.

Before the elevated structure was built

And after….

7 WHITMORE STREET

BUILT: unknown

CLOSED: unknown – Building razed, street non-existent today.

Very little information is available on this location.

Occupied by Ladder 17 temporarily from November 9, 1925 until February 17, 1926 when the company returned to a remodeled firehouse at 157 Harrison Avenue.

Richard Connelly

18 MASON STREET, DOWNTOWN

Built: May 7, 1874

Closed: October 9, 1925 – Building razed

Occupied by Engine 26 from date of organization on May 7, 1874 until October 9, 1925 when they moved to a temporary location at 5 Bulfinch Street (E4)

Engine 26 temporarily relocated to 25 Church Street from July 20, 1920 until January 5, 1921 and again from August 12, 1921 until May 22, 1922.

Occupied by Engine 35, which was organized as a second section of Engine 26 on June 12, 1890 until October 9, 1925 when E35 pumper relocated to 5 Bulfinch Street (E4) and E35 high pressure wagon relocated to 25 Church Street (R1) where it operated as Engine 35.

Occupied by District 5 from May 7, 1874 until May 12, 1905 when they moved to the quarters of Ladder 18 at 9 Pittsburgh Street.

Occupied by District 5 from June 9, 1909 until October 9, 1925 when they relocated to 7 East Street. (E7)

Occupied by the Deputy Chief from date of organization until June 9, 1909 when the division headquarters was moved to Fort Hill Square. (L8)

Occupied by the Chief of Department until October 9, 1925 when the office was relocated to 60 Bristol Street.

18 Mason Street firehouse

Home to Engine 26 and Engine 35

25 CHURCH STREET, BAY VILLAGE

Built: April 1, 1869

Closed: April 17, 1928 – Currently used as a private residence.

Occupied by Hose 8 from April 1, 1869 until April 25, 1874 when Hose 8 was disbanded.

Occupied by Chemical 2 from date of organization on April 25, 1874 until July 20, 1920 when Chemical 2 was disbanded.

Occupied temporarily by Engine 26 from July 20, 1920 until January 5, 1921 when they returned to 18 Mason Street.

Once again occupied temporarily by Engine 26 from August 12, 1921 until May 22, 1922 when they again returned to 18 Mason Street.

Occupied by Rescue 1 from June 5, 1922 until April 17, 1928 when they moved to a new firehouse at 194 Broadway. (E26)

Occupied by Engine 35's High Pressure Wagon from Oct. 9, 1925 until April 17, 1928 when the company moved to a new firehouse at 194 Broadway. (E26)

Note 'Chemical 2' imbedded in the granite lintel still visible over the door

194 BROADWAY, SOUTH END

BUILT: April 17, 1928

CLOSED: May 10, 1971 – Building razed

Occupied by Engine 26 from April 17, 1928 until May 10, 1971.

Occupied by Water Tower 2 from April 17, 1928 until January 23, 1946 when it was relocated to 60 Bristol Street.

Occupied by Engine 35 from April 17, 1928 until the company was deactivated on February 4, 1947.

Occupied by Rescue 1 from April 17, 1928 until November 9, 1954 when the company was disbanded.

Occupied by Water Tower 2 from June 26, 1950 until July 13, 1954 when it was relocated to 123 Oliver Street. (E25)

Occupied by Ladder 17 from January 7, 1946 until May 10, 1971.

Occupied by Engine 7 from July 13, 1954 until May 10, 1971.

Occupied by Engine 10 for one day, February 14, 1946, then the company was relocated to Bowdoin Square.

Occupied by District 5 from April 17, 1928 until August 9, 1939 when the district headquarters moved to 7 East Street. (E7)

Note: Engine 7, Engine 26 and Ladder 17 moved to a new firehouse at 200 Columbus Avenue on May 10, 1971.

Occupied by the office of the Chief of Department. The Chief's quarters even had a fireplace.

The old neighborhood

As demolition was taking place all around them

200 COLUMBUS AVENUE, BACK BAY

Built: May 10, 1971

Still in service

Occupied by Engine 7 from May 10, 1971 until present.

Occupied by Engine 26 from May 10, 1971 until April 10, 1981 when disbanded during Proposition 2 ½.

Occupied by Ladder 17 from May 10, 1971 until October 26, 2005 when Ladder 17 became designated as Tower Ladder 17.

Occupied by Tower Ladder 17 from October 26, 2005 until present.

Occupied by District 4 from May 10, 1971 until present.

Engine 26 was originally quartered here also.

941 BOYLSTON STREET, BACK BAY

Built: February 20, 1888

Still in service

Occupied by Engine 33 from date of organization on February 20, 1888 until present.

Engine 33 and Ladder 15 temporarily located at rear of Fire Alarm Office at 59 The Fenway in a temporary building from November 5, 1970 until September 7, 1971 while their quarters were being renovated.

Occupied by Ladder 15 from date of organization on February 20, 1888 until March 16, 1993 when they were temporarily moved to 700 Tremont Street. (E22)

Occupied by Ladder 15 from September 30, 1993 until present.

Probably Boston's most photographed firehouse

59 THE FENWAY

Built: 1970

Still in service as Fire Alarm Garage

Occupied temporarily by Engine 33 and Ladder 15 from November 5, 1970 until September 7, 1971 in this metal frame building, which was constructed in the rear of the Fire Alarm Office while their quarters were being renovated.

A temporary engine company designated as Engine 6 was in service at Fire Alarm from April 18, 1963 until November 8, 1963 while the Boylston Street over the Massachusetts Turnpike was being reconstructed. This building was not standing during this time.

Occupied by the Mobile Command Post from July 7, 2003 until December 5, 2005 when the unit's designation was changed to Field-Comm.

Occupied by the Field Comm and the Tactical Communications Unit. (Tac-Com)

Various Fire Alarm Construction vehicles are housed here also.

Presently used as a garage for Fire Alarm vehicles

2

South Boston

South Boston (the actual location is east of Boston Proper) can be reached by crossing one of nine bridges. These bridges span waterways and railroad rights-of-way.

You can cross the water by using the Moakley Bridge, the Congress Street Bridge, the Summer Street Bridge, the Broadway Bridge, the West Fourth Street Bridge, or the Malibu Bridge in Dorchester. To cross the railroad one might use the Southampton Street Bridge, the Boston Street Bridge or the Columbia Road Bridge.

In Southie, as it is lovingly known to its residents, you could live in the lower end or at the Point. The lower end is usually thought to be anything west of F Street and the Point (City Point) anything east of L Street. Southie also has four housing developments and a Revolutionary War fort.

Three-deckers, once again, are the mainstay of South Boston's residential core of housing and attached two story houses. There is an extensive waterfront including beaches and shipping facilities, cruise ship docks and a drydock. The area becoming known as the Seaport District is physically in District 6 who commands the South Boston area.

A very interesting fact about Southie is that its streets actually do have a rhyme and reason to the layout. The street grid is basically just that, a grid with the lettered streets running north to south and the numbered streets running east to west. The numbered streets are named from First to Ninth and the lettered streets from A through P with the exception of the letter 'J'.

There are two firehouses housing two engines and two ladders plus the district chief in South Boston. There are also more abandoned firehouses here than in any other section of the city.

WEST BROADWAY near DORCHESTER STREET

Built: Prior to 1859

Closed: April 1868

Building razed and today a block of stores occupies the site.

Occupied by Hand Engine 1 prior to December 19, 1859.

Occupied by Engine 1 from date of organization on December 19, 1859 until April, 1868 when the company moved to a new firehouse at 119 Dorchester Street and this old firehouse was closed.

119 DORCHESTER STREET at W. Fourth Street

Built: April, 1868

Remodeled: June 20, 1917

Closed: April 22, 1977

Building still standing and is presently used as private residences.

Occupied by Engine 1 from April, 1868 until October 30, 1916 when they were temporarily relocated to 456 W. Fourth Street (L5) while Engine 1's quarters were being renovated.

Occupied by Engine 1 from June 20, 1917 until April 22, 1977 when the company was relocated to a newly built firehouse at 272 D Street.

Occupied by Ladder 5 from June 20, 1917 until May 25, 1954 when the company was disbanded.

Temporarily occupied by Ladder 18 from December 27, 1963 until January 6, 1964.

Occupied by District 6 from date of organization on April 7, 1874 until April 22, 1977 when the district headquarters was moved to 272 D Street.

Note: At the time of renovations, the third floor was removed from this firehouse. After abandonment by the BFD, the third floor was restored when the building was converted to condominiums essentially returning the firehouse to its original configuration.

Engine 1's house as it stood before renovations which took off the third and half of the second floors

Today it is used as condominiums

272 D STREET

Built: April 22, 1977

Still in service, the home of Engine 39. Ladder 18, District 6, and the Decon Unit.

Occupied by Engine 1 from April 22, 1977 until April 10, 1981 when the company was deactivated due to Proposition 2 ½.

Occupied by Engine 39 from April 22, 1977 until present.

Occupied by Ladder 18 from April 22, 1977 until present.

Occupied by District 6 from April 22, 1977 until present.

Occupied by Engine 21 temporarily from September 11, 1995 until January 27, 1996 when they returned to their own quarters at 641 Columbia Road.

Occupied by the Mobile Command Post from November 1996 until July 7, 2003 when the unit relocated to 59 the Fenway. (Fire Alarm Office)

Occupied by the Haz Mat Unit (H3) from September 26, 2001 until November 1, 2001 when the Haz-Mat Unit was relocated to 700 Tremont Street. (E22)

Occupied by Decon Unit (H7) until present.

This D Street firehouse once also housed Engine 1

715 EAST FOURTH STREET between K and L Streets

Built: 1857

Closed: May 2, 1932

Still standing. Currently used as a Veterans' Post.

Occupied by Hand Engine 14 in November, 1857

Occupied by Engine 2 from date of organization on September 17, 1860 until May 10, 1882 when the company moved to 863 East Fourth Street at O Street.

Occupied by Hose 12 from May 10, 1882 until the company was disbanded and reorganized as Combination Wagon 2 on May 10, 1893.

Occupied by Combination Wagon 2 from date of organization on May 10, 1893 until April 21, 1905 when the company was reorganized as Ladder Company 19.

Occupied by Ladder 19 from April 21, 1905 until May 2, 1932 when the company was relocated to a new firehouse at 700 East Fourth Street.

Engine 2's firehouse before Ladder
19 took over here

Today a veteran's post occupies the
old firehouse

863 EAST FOURTH STREET at O Street

Built: June 17, 1873

Closed: May 3, 1932

Currently used as a veterans post and formerly used as storage for the BFD carpenter shop.

Occupied by Hose 12 from date of organization on June 17, 1873 until May 10, 1882 when the company was relocated to 715 East Fourth Street between K and L Streets.

Occupied by Engine 2 from May 10, 1882 until May 3, 1932 when the company was relocated to new quarters at 700 East Fourth Street.

This view shows Engine 2 as it stood when it was occupied as a firehouse

Today this is Engine 2's former firehouse at 863 E. Fourth Street

700 EAST FOURTH STREET

Built: May 2, 1932

Still in service, the home of Engine 2 and Ladder 19.

Occupied by Ladder 19 from May 2, 1932 until present.

Occupied by Engine 2 from May 3, 1932 until present.

Occupied by Lighting Plant 1 and Fuel Wagon 1 from December 8, 1937 for an unspecified short time.

An earlier view of Engine 2 and Ladder 19

Engine 2 and Ladder 19 today with the drill tower in the rear yard

456 WEST FOURTH STREET

Built: December 22, 1869

Closed: June 21, 1917

Building still standing. Currently used as a Veterans' Post

Occupied by Engine 15 from date of organization on December 22, 1869 until sometime in 1871 when the company moved to a new firehouse at 109 Dorchester Avenue at West Broadway.

Occupied by Ladder 5 from date of organization circa January 1, 1870 until June 20, 1917 when company was relocated to 119 Dorchester Street with Engine 1.

Temporarily occupied by Engine 1 from October 30, 1916 until June 20, 1917 while the firehouse at 119 Dorchester Street was being remodeled.

Note: Still visible above the door are the letters "Hook and Ladder 5".

This is Ladder 5's old firehouse

109 DORCHESTER AVENUE at West Broadway

Built: March 1872

Closed: July 13, 1954

Building razed: circa 1990. The area today is rehabbed into a new roadway and bridge.

Occupied by Engine 15 from 1871 until July 2, 1917 when the company was temporarily moved to 116 B Street at Athens Street while the subway tunnel was being constructed under their quarters.

Occupied by Engine 15 from December 15, 1917 until July 13, 1954 when the company was disbanded and the firehouse abandoned.

An early view of Engine 15 with two doors, before motorized apparatus

A later photo after renovations….and now the firehouse is just a memory

116 B STREET at Athens Street

Built: November 1, 1860

Closed: December 15, 1917

Still standing and is currently occupied by a private business.

Occupied by Horse Hose 9 from date of organization on November 1, 1860 until October 27, 1887 when the company was disbanded.

Occupied by Chemical Engine 8 from date of organization on October 27, 1887 until July 2, 1917 when the company was disbanded.

Temporarily occupied by Engine 15 from July 2, 1917 until December 15, 1917 when they moved back into their own quarters at 109 Dorchester Avenue.

A plastics firm occupies the old Chemical 8 firehouse in South Boston

9 PITTSBURGH STREET (Now known as Thomson Place)

Built: November 7, 1902

Closed: November 17, 1953

Building razed – Vacant lot today

This firehouse had a pole that went from the third floor to the main floor as opposed to two separate poles with one from the third floor to second floor and another from the second floor to the main floor.

Occupied by Ladder 18 from date of organization on November 7, 1902 until November 17, 1953 when Ladder 18 was relocated to 344 Congress Street with Engine 39.

Occupied by Water Tower 3 from date of organization on November 2, 1903 until the company was disbanded on August 9, 1939.

Occupied once again by Water Tower 3 when it was reactivated on March 27, 1946 until again disbanded on February 4, 1947.

Occupied temporarily by Engine 25 from September 26, 1952 until September 11, 1953 when the company moved into the new firehouse at 123 Oliver Street.

Occupied by District 5 from May 12, 1905 until June 9, 1909 when the district headquarters was relocated to 18 Mason Street. (E26-E35)

Occupied by District 3 from June 9, 1909 until August 8, 1939 when District 3 was abolished.

Occupied by District 3 once again upon their re-establishment on June 5, 1946 until May 4, 1954 when District 3 was relocated to the Bowdoin Square firehouse. (E4)

This firehouse location is another vacant lot today

Richard Connelly

344 CONGRESS STREET

Built: May 18, 1891

Closed: April 22, 1977

Currently occupied by the Boston Fire Museum and the Boston Sparks Association, the organization that runs the museum.

Occupied by Engine 38-39 from date of organization on May 18, 1891 until February 4, 1947 when Engine 38 was deactivated.

Occupied by Engine 39 until April 22, 1977.

Occupied temporarily by Ladder 8 from September 26, 1952 until September 11, 1953 when the company was relocated to the new firehouse at 123 Oliver Street.

Occupied by Ladder 18 from November 17, 1953 until April 22, 1977.

Engine 39 and Ladder 18 moved to a newly constructed firehouse at 272 D Street on April 22, 1977.

This is what the firehouse looked like when the area was known as the wool district

Today it is home to the Boston Fire Museum

330 DORCHESTER STREET at JENKINS STREET

Built: Prior to November 1, 1861

Closed: November 13, 1893

Currently used as a union hall.

Occupied by Hand Hose 10 from date of organization on November 1, 1861 until March 1, 1868 when the company was reorganized as Horse Hose Company 10.

Occupied by Horse Hose Company 10 from date of organization on March 1, 1868 until November 13, 1893 when this firehouse was closed and the company was disbanded and reorganized as Engine Company 43 in a new firehouse at 5 Boston Street in Andrew Square.

At one time Hose 10 occupied this structure

5 BOSTON STREET at Andrew Square

Built: November 13, 1893

Closed: July 1, 1961

Used as a private business until the building was razed in late 1970s. A portion of this property is currently occupied by a parking lot for a bank.

Occupied by Engine 43 from date of organization on November 13, 1893 until July 1, 1961 when the company was relocated to the former quarters of Engine 23 at 900 Massachusetts Avenue.

Occupied by Combination Ladder 3 from date of organization on January 7, 1898 until April 21, 1905 when the company was reorganized as Ladder Company 20.

Occupied by Ladder 20 from April 21, 1905 until July 1, 1961 when the company was relocated to 900 Massachusetts Avenue and this firehouse was abandoned.

Occupied temporarily by Engine 21 Wagon from July 18, 1925 until February 17, 1926 when the new firehouse opened at 641 Columbia Road.

Today this old firehouse is a vacant lot. This was the first firehouse I ever stepped foot into

920 MASSACHUSETTS AVENUE
(Original address was 900 Massachusetts Avenue)

Built: August 20, 1951

Still in service as a fire department facility

Occupied by Engine 23 from August 20, 1951 until July 13, 1954 when the company was disbanded.

Occupied by Lighting Plant 2 from August 20, 1951 until July 13, 1954 when the Lighting Plant was moved to 618 Harrison Avenue with (E3)

Occupied by Engine 43 from July 1, 1961 until February 4, 1981 when the company was disbanded due to proposition 2 ½.

Occupied by Ladder 20 from July 1, 1961 until February 4, 1981 when the company was disbanded due to Proposition 2 ½.

Occupied by the Fire Investigation Unit from 1981 until present.

Note: Address was changed on June 5, 1962.

Built as engine 23's quarters, it later became the home of Engine 43, Ladder 20. Today it houses the Fire Investigation unit

3

East Boston

East Boston (originally known as Noddle's Island and is actually north of Boston Proper) is separated from the city by Boston Harbor. Up until recently, there were two tunnels to reach East Boston. Boston to East Boston traffic traveled through the Callahan Tunnel and the opposite flow of traffic used the Sumner Tunnel. In 1995, the Ted Williams Tunnel to East Boston opened. This tunnel and roadway is actually an extension of the Massachusetts Turnpike (I-90).

Before these tunnels existed, it was necessary to take the ferry to get to the other side. When the Sumner Tunnel opened in 1934, it signaled the end of the ferry service between Boston and East Boston. Traffic traveled in one lane in either direction until 1961, when the Callahan Tunnel opened.

There is actually a fourth tunnel which carries the MBTA Blue Line trains back and forth although no foot or vehicle traffic uses it.

Logan International Airport is situated in Eastie, as it is familiarly known to its residents. Many docks, piers and waterfront lots face Boston Harbor. There are numerous petroleum storage facilities in the district. Once again, many three-deckers line the streets as well as two story single family homes.

Three firehouses are in the district today housing three engines, two ladders and the district chief of District 1. District 1 is in Division One.

MERIDIAN STREET

Built: unknown

Closed: January 1, 1866 – building razed

Not a lot of information is available about this location.

Occupied by Hand Engine 10 for an undetermined period.

Occupied by Ladder 2 from date of organization on October 1, 1849 until January 1, 1866 when the company was relocated to 260 Sumner Street and the Meridian Street firehouse was abandoned.

391 CHELSEA STREET

Built: 1857

Closed: September 21, 1902 – Abandoned and razed

Site occupied by a restaurant today

Occupied by Horse Hose 6 from September 1, 1860 until May 18, 1891 when the company was disbanded.

Occupied by Chemical Engine 7 from May 18, 1891 until September 21, 1902 when the company moved to 360 Saratoga Street and the Chelsea Street firehouse was abandoned.

Today a fine Italian restaurant occupies the former firehouse site at 391 Chelsea Street

64 MARION ST. between Eutaw and Trenton Sts.

Built: September 1, 1860

Closed: October 4, 1917 – Building razed for a new firehouse to be built on this site.

Occupied by Engine 5 from September 1, 1860 until October 4, 1917 when they were temporarily relocated to 360 Saratoga Street with Ladder 31.

Occupied by Ladder 2 temporarily from May 18, 1891 until October 27, 1892 when they were relocated to 60 Paris Street. (E9)

64 MARION STREET (2nd firehouse at this location)

Built: September 27, 1919

Closed: September 21, 1938

Presently used as a private residence

Occupied by Engine 5 from September 27, 1919 until September 21, 1938 when they were permanently relocated to 360 Saratoga Street.

Occupied by District 1 from September 16, 1927 until September 21, 1938 when the district headquarters was moved to 360 Saratoga Street.

64 Marion Street firehouse when it was in service

Today it has been remodeled into an apartment house

Richard Connelly

360 SARATOGA STREET at Prescott Street

Built: September 21, 1902

Still in service, home to Engine 5 and District 1. This building has seen extensive remodeling in recent years.

Occupied by Chemical Engine 7 from September 21, 1902 until June 14, 1926 when the company was disbanded.

Occupied by Ladder 31 from date of organization on June 14, 1926 until the company was disbanded on May 25, 1954.

Occupied by Engine 5 temporarily from October 4, 1917 until September 27, 1919 when they returned to a newly built firehouse at 64 Marion Street.

Occupied by Ladder 21 temporarily from December 1, 1927 until February 7, 1928 when they returned to their own quarters.

Occupied by Engine 5 from September 21, 1938 until February 8, 1999 when they temporarily moved to 239 Sumner Street while this firehouse at 360 Saratoga Street was being remodeled.

Occupied by Engine 5 from October 7, 1999 until present.

Occupied by Engine Squad 11 from July 1, 1961 until July 14, 1969 when the company became designated as Engine 11 again.

Occupied by Engine 11 from July 14, 1969 until October 20, 1981 when the company was disbanded due to Proposition 2 ½.

Occupied by Engine 9 temporarily from August 14, 1930 until January 21, 1931 when they returned to 60 Paris Street.

Occupied by Engine 40 temporarily from October 3, 1923 until November 8, 1924 when they returned to 260 Sumner Street.

Occupied by District 1 from September 21, 1938 until February 8, 1999 when they temporarily moved to 239 Sumner Street while quarters were being remodeled.

Occupied by District 1 from October 7, 1999 until present.

Note: When Engine 11 was put out of service on October 20, 1981, a group of concerned citizens moved into the firehouse and would not let the Fire Department remove Engine 11 from quarters. This action would continue for many months before finally, one night the fire engine was whisked away when only one or two people were in quarters.

Firehouse on Saratoga Street as it was built for Ladder 31

Engine 5's quarters as it stands today at 360 Saratoga Street

60 PARIS STREET

Built: Prior to December 26, 1859

Closed: May 16, 1977

Presently used as a social club.

Occupied by Extinguisher Wagon 3 from date of organization on August 24, 1872 until May 21, 1874 when the company was disbanded.

Occupied by Hose 11 from September 17, 1872 until an undetermined date.

Occupied by Engine 9 from December 26, 1859 until August 14, 1930 when the company was temporarily moved to 360 Saratoga Street. (L31)

Again occupied by Engine 9 from January 21, 1931 until May 16, 1977 when a new firehouse opened at 239 Sumner Street.

Occupied by Ladder 2 from October 27, 1892 until August 14, 1930 when the company was temporarily moved to 260 Sumner Street. (E40)

Again occupied by Ladder 2 from January 21, 1931 until May 16, 1977 when a new firehouse opened at 239 Sumner St.

Occupied by District 1 from date organization on April 7, 1874 until September 16, 1927 when District 1 was relocated to 64 Marion Street with Engine 5.

This is an early photo of Engine 9 and Ladder 2 at 60 Paris Street

This how it looked as I knew it

Today it is occupied by an Italian-American club

761 SARATOGA STREET at Byron Street

Built: September 27, 1886

Closed: July 1, 1961 – Abandoned and razed.

Today there is a playground dedicated to Engine 11 on the site.

Occupied by Chemical Engine 7 from date of organization on September 27, 1886 until May 18, 1891 when the company was relocated to 391 Chelsea Street.

Occupied by Engine 11 from date of organization on May 18, 1891 until November 15, 1950 when they temporarily occupied the newly built firehouse at 1 Ashley Street prior to the organization of Engine 56.

On May 9, 1951 Engine 11 returned to 761 Saratoga Street. On September 21, 1954 Engine 11 was designated as Engine Squad 11 and remained at 761 Saratoga Street until July 1, 1961 when the company was relocated to 360 Saratoga Street. (E5) This firehouse was abandoned by the city.

Occupied by Combination Ladder 4 from date of organization December 24, 1897 until April 21, 1905 when reorganized as Ladder 21.

Occupied by Ladder 21 from April 21, 1905 until December 1, 1927 when they moved temporarily to 360 Saratoga Street (E5)

Occupied by Ladder 21 from February 7, 1928 until July 1, 1961 when they moved to the firehouse at 1 Ashley Street leaving this firehouse empty.

Engine 11's firehouse when it was in service

This playground is on the site of old Engine 11's house

260 SUMNER STREET at Orleans Street

Built: January 1, 1866

Closed: October 3, 1923

Razed for new firehouse to be built on this site.

Occupied by Chemical 7 from date of organization on until May 18, 1891 when they relocated to the quarters of Hose 6 at 391 Chelsea Street.

Occupied by Engine 11 from date of organization on January 1, 1866 until May 18, 1891 when they moved to 761 Saratoga Street.

Occupied by Ladder 2 from January 1, 1866 until May 18, 1891 when they temporarily moved to 64 Marion Street. (E5)

Occupied by newly organized Engine 40 from May 18, 1891 until October 3, 1923 when they were temporarily relocated to 360 Saratoga Street while a new firehouse was being constructed at 260 Sumner Street for Engine 40.

Original firehouse at 260 Sumner Street

260 SUMNER STREET (second firehouse at this site)

Built: November 8, 1924

Closed: May 13, 1977

Still standing - vacant

Occupied by Engine 40 from November 8, 1924 until May 13, 1977 when they moved to a new firehouse at 239 Sumner Street.

Occupied by Engine 9 temporarily from November 20, 1976 until December 13, 1976 when the company returned to 60 Paris Street.

Occupied by Ladder 2 temporarily from August 14, 1930 until January 21, 1931 when they returned to 60 Paris Street.

The firehouse at 260 Sumner Street when it was built

As I remember Engine 40's house when it was in service

As the building stands today

239 SUMNER STREET between Railroad and Orleans Street

Built: May 13, 1977

Still in service as quarters for Engine 9 and Ladder 2.

Occupied by Engine 9 from May 16, 1977 until present.

Occupied by Ladder 2 from May 16, 1977 until November 6, 2005 when Ladder 2 became designated as Tower Ladder 2.

Occupied by Tower Ladder 2 from November 6, 2005 until March 2007 when the company once again became Ladder 2.

Occupied by Ladder from March 2007 until present.

Occupied by Engine 40 from May 13, 1977 until April 10, 1981 when the company was disbanded due to Proposition 2 ½.

Occupied temporarily by Engine 5 and District 1 from February 8, 1999 until October 7, 1999 while their firehouse at 360 Saratoga Street was being remodeled.

This present day firehouse once quartered Engine 40 also

1 ASHLEY STREET

Built: November 15, 1950

Still in service, home to Engine 56 and Ladder 21.

Occupied by Engine 11 temporarily from November 15, 1950 until May 9, 1951 when the company returned to 761 Saratoga Street.

Occupied by the newly organized Engine 56 from May 9, 1951 until present.

Occupied by Ladder 21 from July 1, 1961 until present.

Note: This firehouse was originally built with one large overhead door. A remodeling project transformed this firehouse into a two door firehouse in early 1990s.

This firehouse was built with one large door and remained that way even after Ladder 21 moved in

Today the single door has been replaced with two doors

4

Roxbury

Another once beautiful section of the City of Boston is Roxbury. Roxbury consists of Roxbury, Roxbury Highlands, Mission Hill, and Roxbury Crossing. You will find massive wood frame dwellings in this area, which were once single family homes. They have been broken up into two, three, and occasionally four family homes. In the late nineteenth and early twentieth century, many of the elite in the city resided in Roxbury, however it was primarily a working class neighborhood.

Roxbury went through a tough time in the 1950s, 60s, and 70s. Fires tore through the area. Many once beautiful and stately mansions were burned and destroyed.

Roxbury has many three-deckers with peaked roofs, making 3½ story wood framed dwellings.

Roxbury was also home to many manufacturing and mercantile plants. Breweries abounded both in Roxbury and Jamaica Plain. Streetcar lines traversed every main street to bring the residents into the downtown area to work and shop. Many hospitals were also located here.

Today three firehouses which house three engines, two ladders, a rescue company and two district chiefs are all that is left in the district. Many firehouses were once in this district with companies being either disbanded or placed together occupying the same firehouse.

DUDLEY AND WARREN STREETS

Built: Prior to September 9, 1864

Closed: An unspecified date in 1873 – Building later razed

Occupied by a Roxbury Steam Engine Co. from September 9, 1864 until January 6, 1868 when Roxbury was annexed to Boston. The Roxbury Steam Engine Company was reorganized as Engine 12.

Occupied by Engine 12 from January 6, 1868 until November 20, 1873 when the company moved into a new firehouse at 198 Dudley Street.

This original Roxbury firehouse was situated in today's Dudley Square

20 EUSTIS STREET

Built: Prior to January 6, 1868

Closed: October 2, 1916

Still standing, vacant.

Occupied by a Roxbury Ladder Company from a date prior to January 6, 1868. When Roxbury was annexed to Boston on January 6, 1868 the company continued to occupy these quarters until an unspecified date in 1869 when the Roxbury Ladder Company was reorganized as Ladder 4.

Occupied by Ladder 4 from sometime in 1869 until May 1874 when the company moved to a new firehouse at 407 Dudley Street.

Occupied temporarily by Ladder 4 from December 27, 1878 until October 30, 1880 when they were relocated to 198 Dudley Street.

Occupied by Ladder 4 temporarily from January 16, 1916 until October 2, 1916 when they again returned to 198 Dudley Street.

Occupied by Chemical 10 from date of organization on September 16, 1889 until January 17, 1916 when the company was temporarily put out of service until returning to service at 198 Dudley Street on October 2, 1916.

Occupied temporarily by Ladder 4 from January 17, 1916 until October 2, 1916 when they returned to 198 Dudley Street.

When the old firehouse at 20 Eustis Street was in service

As the building looks today

198 DUDLEY STREET at WINSLOW STREET

Built: November 20, 1873

Closed: December 23, 1974

Building stood vacant until razed in the mid 1980s and remains a vacant lot today.

Occupied by Engine 12 from November 20, 1873 until September 30, 1880 when they moved to 407 Dudley Street.

Again occupied by Engine 12 temporarily from August 15, 1924 until January 7, 1925 when they again returned to 407 Dudley Street.

Occupied once more by Engine 12 from September 21, 1938 until October 16, 1946 when they returned to 407 Dudley Street.

Occupied by Ladder 4 from October 30, 1880 until January 17, 1916 when they were temporarily relocated to 20 Eustis Street.

Again occupied by Ladder 4 from October 2, 1916 where they remained until July 21, 1965 when Ladder 4 was again temporarily relocated to 407 Dudley Street.

Occupied again by Ladder 4 from August 2, 1965 until December 23, 1974 when they moved to a new firehouse at 174 Dudley Street with Engines 12, 14 and District 13.

Occupied by Chemical 10 when it was restored to service on October 2, 1916 until July 28, 1922 when company was disbanded.

Occupied by Foamite Unit 1 from November 26, 1926 until December 10, 1926 when it was reorganized as Rescue Co. 2.

Occupied by Rescue Co. 2 from December 10, 1926 until September 21, 1938 when they moved to 27 Centre Street. (E14)

Occupied temporarily by Engine 23 from May 16, 1949 until August 20, 1951 when they relocated to new quarters at 900 Massachusetts Avenue.

Occupied by Division 2 from June 9, 1909 until September 14, 1913 when a third Division was established and Division 2 headquarters was relocated to 70 Warren Avenue. (E22)

Division 3 was established and located here from September 14, 1913 until it was abolished on March 14, 1914 and this firehouse was again occupied by Division 2.
Occupied by Division 2 once again, from March 14, 1914 until July 5, 1919.

Division 3 was again in service and quartered here from July 5, 1919 until May 4, 1922 when the division headquarters was moved to 36 Washington Street. (L23)

Occupied by District 9 from date of organization on April 7, 1874 until June 9, 1909 when they were relocated to 407 Dudley St. (E12)

Again occupied by District 9 from September 21, 1938 until October 16, 1946 when they once again moved to 407 Dudley Street.

This was the last fire station in Boston to be occupied by a single ladder truck.

Apparently a holiday, perhaps July 4th

As I remember Ladder 4's house in the 1960s

407 DUDLEY STREET

Built: 1873

Closed: December 18, 1974

Building still standing, used as a Spanish community center.

Occupied by Ladder 4 from May 1874 until December 27, 1878 when they returned to 20 Eustis Street.

Occupied by Ladder 4 temporarily from July 21, 1965 until August 2, 1965 when they returned to 198 Dudley Street.

Occupied by Engine 12 from September 30, 1880 until August 15, 1924 when they were temporarily relocated back to 198 Dudley Street.

Occupied by Engine 12 from January 7, 1925 until September 21, 1938 when they moved back to 198 Dudley Street.

Occupied again by Engine 12 from October 16, 1946 where they remained until December 18, 1974 when they moved to a new firehouse at 174 Dudley Street with Engine 14, Ladder 4 and District 13.

Occupied by District 9 from June 9, 1909 until September 21, 1938 when they were relocated to 198 Dudley Street. (L4)

Again occupied by District 9 from October 16, 1946 until May 4, 1954 when District 9 and District 8 were consolidated into one district, District 5, which was relocated to 560 Huntington Avenue. (E37)

Occupied by District 13 (Special Service Unit) from 1976 until December 18, 1974 when they moved to a new firehouse at 174 Dudley Street. (E14)

Note: Firehouse at 407 Dudley Street used as paint shop from September 21, 1938 until October 16, 1946 when Engine 12 returned.

When Engine 12 still ran out of this firehouse

Today a Spanish Community Center is housed here

Richard Connelly

174 DUDLEY STREET

Built: December 18, 1974

Still in service and houses Engine 14, Ladder 4 and The Safety Chief (H1).

Occupied by Engine 12 from December 18, 1974 until April 10, 1981 when Engine 12 was deactivated.

Occupied by Engine 14 from December 19, 1974 until present.

Occupied by Ladder 4 from December 23, 1974 until present.

Occupied by District 13 (Special Services Chief) from December 18, 1974 until 1981 when District 13 deactivated due to Proposition 2 ½.

Temporarily occupied by Engine 37 from June 1, 1995 until November 6, 1995 while the firehouse at 560 Huntington Avenue was being remodeled.

Occupied by the Safety Division Chief (H1) from June 20, 2001 until present.

Engines 12, 14, Ladder 4 and the Special Service Unit (Car 13) were originally housed here at 174 Dudley Street

185 CABOT STREET

Built: Prior to January 6, 1868

Closed: 1872

Building razed and a public housing project occupies the site today.

Occupied by a Roxbury Hose Company prior to August 1, 1860.

Occupied by Hose 7 from date of organization on January 6, 1868 until an unknown date in February 1872 when the company moved to 1046 Tremont St. (L12)

201 CABOT at CULVERT (WHITTIER) STREETS

Built: April 6, 1865

Closed: April 21, 1938

Building stood vacant for years until razed in the late 60s. A public school occupies the site today.

Occupied by a Roxbury Steam Engine from April 6, 1865 until January 6, 1868 when Roxbury was annexed to Boston.

Occupied by Engine 13 from date of annexation and reorganization on January 6, 1868 until April 21, 1938 when they moved to 1046 Tremont St. (L12).

As the old Engine 13 firehouse originally sat

As the neighborhood changed

As I remembered this building in the 1960s

1046 TREMONT STREET (1)

Built: unspecified date in 1871

Destroyed: May 15, 1894

Note: Firehouse destroyed during "Roxbury conflagration". An apartment complex sits on this parcel of land today.

Occupied by Hose 7 from February 1872 until December 22, 1891 when they were temporarily located at a stable on Northampton Street.

Occupied by Ladder 12 from date of organization on July 31, 1880 until January 16, 1892 when they moved to a temporary location in a stable on Northampton Street while their quarters were being renovated.

Occupied by Ladder 12 from January 16, 1892 until the firehouse was destroyed by fire in the "Roxbury Conflagration" on May 15, 1894.

Note: Companies temporarily relocated to a location on Culvert St. (Whittier St.)

NORTHAMPTON STREET CAR HOUSE

Not much information available

Occupied by Hose 7 from December 22, 1891 until May15, 1894 when they were relocated to a temporary quarters at Culvert street at Hampshire Street.

CULVERT STREET at Hampshire Street

Built: Unknown

Closed: 1896

Building razed, street non-existent today.

Very little information available for this location.

Occupied by Hose 7 from May 15, 1894 until April 6, 1896 when the company was disbanded.

Occupied temporarily by Ladder 12 from May 15, 1894 until September 1896 when they moved back to a new firehouse at 1046 Tremont Street.

1046 TREMONT STREET (2)

Built: September 1896

Closed: June 11, 1960 – Abandoned by the city.

Building used as quarters of the Boston Fire Patrol, a privately owned salvage company, until razed, circa 1972. Benjamin A. Ellis, famed Boston fire buff, owned this business which boarded up buildings after fires. An apartment building sits on this parcel of land today.

Occupied by Ladder 12 from September 1896 until June 11, 1960 when the company was deactivated.

Occupied by Chemical 12 from date of organization on October 8, 1896 until August 30, 1918 when the company was disbanded.

Occupied by Engine 13 from April 21, 1938 until June 11, 1960 when they moved to 36 Washington St., Dorchester (L23).

Occupied by Division 2 until June 9, 1909 when they were relocated to 198 Dudley Street. (L4)

Occupied by District 8 from date of organization on April 7, 1874 until October 11, 1933 when the district headquarters moved to 560 Huntington Avenue. (E37)

This firehouse saw much action when Ladder 12 lived here

After the firehouse closed, the Boston Fire Patrol worked out of here

27 CENTRE STREET

Built: Prior to January 6, 1868

Closed: December 19, 1974

Still standing - Building was used as a community center and now stands vacant.

Occupied by Engine 14 from January 6, 1868 when Roxbury was annexed to Boston until February 3, 1916 when they were relocated to a temporary quarters on Linwood Street while this firehouse was renovated.

Occupied by Engine 14 from August 12, 1916 until September 21, 1954 when the company was designated as Engine Squad 14.

Temporarily occupied by Ladder 30 from December 16, 1926 until they returned to 3089 Washington Street on April 1, 1927.

Occupied by Engine Squad 14 from September 21, 1954 until June 13, 1969 when the company again became known as Engine 14.

Occupied by Engine 14 from June 13, 1969 until December 19, 1974 when they moved to new firehouse at 174 Dudley St. with Engine 12, Ladder 4, and District 13.

Occupied by Rescue 2 from September 21, 1938 until September 21, 1954 when the company was disbanded.

Occupied by Lighting Plant 2 from April 26, 1967 until December 16, 1974 when the Lighting Plant moved to 641 Columbia Rd. (E21)

This photo depicts the complement of members in the 1890s

In the 1960s Engine 14 was an extraordinarily busy firehouse

As the old firehouse at 27 Centre Street looks today while awaiting its next assignment

LINWOOD STREET

No information available as to where or what type of building Engine 14 occupied while their quarters at 27 Centre Street were being remodeled from February 3, 1916 until August 12, 1916.

84 NORTHAMPTON STREET

Built: Prior to August 18, 1860

Closed: March 28, 1948

Building razed in the 70s. An apartment complex occupies this area today.

Occupied by Hand Hose 4 prior to August 18, 1860 when reorganized as Horse Hose 4.

Occupied by Horse Hose 4 from date of organization on August 18, 1860 until April 7, 1873 when Engine 23 was organized.

Occupied by Engine 23 from date of organization on April 7, 1873 until this fire station was closed on March 28, 1948 and the company was relocated to a temporary location at 70 Warren Ave. (E22).

Another firehouse with streetcar tracks running in front of it

In the 1970s, before being demolished

434 WARREN STREET

Built: December 10, 1873

Closed: October 25, 1972

Building used as a community center, still standing.

Occupied by Engine 24 from date of organization on December 10, 1873 until November 25, 1946 when they were relocated temporarily to 36 Washington St. (L23).

On March 27, 1947 Engine 24 returned to its own quarters where they remained until October 25, 1972 when they moved to 36 Washington Street and the fire station at 434 Warren Street was abandoned.

Note: Building originally had two overhead doors and was renovated and converted to a single door firehouse in 1961.

As a neighborhood firehouse

Richard Connelly

Today it houses a youth center

352 LONGWOOD AVENUE

Built: July 27, 1874

Closed: October 11, 1933

Building still stands and used as a florist shop, overhead door lintels still visible.

Occupied by Chemical 3 when organized on July 27, 1874 until October 4, 1901 when the company was disbanded.

Occupied by Engine 37 from date of organization on September 16, 1890 until October 11, 1933 when they moved to a new firehouse at 560 Huntington Avenue.

Occupied by Combination Ladder 10 from date of organization on October 4, 1901 until April 21, 1905 when the company was disbanded.

Occupied by Ladder 26 from date of organization on April 21, 1905 until October 11, 1933 when they moved to a new firehouse at 560 Huntington Avenue.

The companies formerly quartered here would become the city's busiest after they moved to 560 Huntington Avenue

Today it is a florist shop in the hospital area. Children's Beth Israel, Deaconess, Dana Farber are but a few of the local hospitals.

560 HUNTINGTON AVENUE

Built: October 11, 1933

Still in service and occupied by Engine 37, Ladder 26, and District 5.

Occupied by Engine 37 from October 11, 1933 until June 1, 1995 when they moved temporarily to 174 Dudley Street.

Occupied by Engine 37 from November 6, 1995 until present.

Occupied by Ladder 26 from October 11, 1933 until November 18, 1970 when Ladder 26 was deactivated. Company reorganized as Aerial Tower 2.

Occupied by Aerial Tower 2 from November 18, 1970 until February 4, 1977 when Aerial Tower 2 was deactivated and Ladder 26 reorganized.

Occupied by Ladder 26 from February 4, 1977 until June 1, 1995 when they moved temporarily to 700 Tremont Street. (E22)

Occupied by Ladder 26 from November 6, 1995 until present.

Occupied by District 8 from October 11, 1933 until May 4, 1954 when District 8 and District 5 were consolidated into one district which became District 5.

Occupied by District 5 from May 4, 1954 until present.

This photo was taken when the District 8 chief resided here

Today it is home to District 5, Engine 37 and Ladder 26

15 WALNUT PARK

Built: Unavailable

Closed: June 1, 1876

Occupied by Chemical 5 at this temporary location from date of organization on November 21, 1874 until they moved to new quarters on Washington Street adjacent to number 3089 on June 1, 1876.

Ladder 30 temporarily located here from August 6, 1926 until December 16, 1926 when they were relocated to 27 Centre Street. (E14)

WASHINGTON STREET adjacent to 3089.

Built: June 1, 1876

Closed: October 27, 1892

Building razed

Occupied by Chemical 5 from June 1, 1876 until October 27, 1892 when they moved to a newly built firehouse next door at 3089 Washington Street.

3089 WASHINGTON STREET

Built: October 27, 1892

Closed: December 19, 1952

Remained vacant until razed in early 70s. Today a public park sits on the site.

Occupied by Chemical 5 from October 27, 1892 until the company was disbanded on March 5, 1913.

Occupied by Ladder 30 from date of organization on March 5, 1913 until August 6, 1926 when they were temporarily relocated to 15 Walnut Park.

Occupied by Ladder 30 again from April 1, 1927 until December 19, 1952 when the company relocated to a new firehouse at 1870 Columbus Avenue.

Occupied by Engine 42 from date of organization on February 10, 1893 until August 6, 1926 when they were temporarily relocated at 36 Washington Street. (L23)

Occupied by Engine 42 from April 1, 1927 until December 19, 1952 when the company relocated to a new firehouse at 1870 Columbus Avenue.

Notice how the firehouse sat on an angle to the street

After the elevated tracks were built

1870 COLUMBUS AVENUE

Built: December 19, 1952

Still in service, occupied by Engine 42, Rescue 2, and District 9.

Occupied by Engine 42 from December 19, 1952 until present.

Occupied by Ladder 30 from December 19, 1952 until April 10, 1981 when the company was disbanded due to Proposition 2 ½.

Occupied by Division 2 from March 31, 1954 until December 18, 1984 when they moved to a new firehouse at 746 Centre Street. (E28)

Occupied by Rescue 2 from April 10, 1981 until January 14, 1982 when the company was disbanded due to Proposition 2 ½.

Occupied by Rescue 2 again, from the date of their reorganization on June 9, 1986 until present.

Temporarily occupied by Pumper unit of Rescue-Pumper, from October 29, 1970 until November 6, 1970.

Occupied by District 9 from December 18, 1984 until present.

When built it had a flat front and ugly solid doors

In the 1960s a patrol room area was added to the front (always cold in the winter)

Today this firehouse houses Engine 42 and Rescue 2

5

Dorchester

The Dorchester section of Boston was originally the Town of Dorchester. On January 3, 1870, after a vote by the City of Boston and the Town of Dorchester, this area was annexed into the City of Boston. Portions of Dorchester are known as Popes Hill, Port Norfolk, Grove Hall, Lower Mills, Neponset, Fields Corner, Savin Hill, Uphams Corner, Adams Village, Four Corners, Meeting House Hill, and Mattapan.

Along with the streets, land and buildings, etc., six engine companies and two ladder companies which were housed in seven firehouses became Boston Fire Department resources. The companies were renumbered as you will see in the following chapter. Presently, all but one of these companies still exists.

The engine companies are Engine 16, 17, 18, 19, 20, and 21. The ladder companies are Ladder 6 and 7. Today, the entire area is covered by District Fire Chiefs in Districts 7 and 8.

Dorchester is basically a residential neighborhood with a moderate sprinkling of mercantile, manufacturing and waterfront properties. Many of the residences are the famed "three deckers". These are three-family, three floor wood framed buildings which house three families in similar floor plan occupancies. Most were built around the turn of the 20th century and early 1900s.

2 TEMPLE STREET

Built: Prior to January 3, 1870 when Dorchester annexed to Boston

Closed: August 12, 1958 – Continued as a firehouse for Civil Defense Engine Company CD10.

Razed: December 22, 1971 after two alarm fire destroyed the building (Two alarms on box 3572). The lot has never been developed.

Occupied by Dorchester Engine 1 prior to January 3, 1870 when the company became Engine 16.

Occupied by Engine 16 from date of organization on January 3, 1870 until August 12, 1958 when the company moved temporarily to 1884 Dorchester Avenue.

Occupied by Civil Defense Engine Company CD-10 (Auxiliary) from an indefinite date until October 1969 when the company was disbanded.

51 River Street and 2 Temple Street, Dorchester

51 RIVER STREET

Built: Prior to January 3, 1870 when Dorchester annexed to Boston

Closed: June 1, 1938

Destroyed by fire: December 22, 1971 (Two alarms on box 3572)

Today this site is a grassed lot, never developed.

Occupied by Dorchester Ladder 1 until the company became Ladder 6 on January 3, 1870.

Occupied by Ladder 6 from date of organization on January 3, 1870 until June 1, 1938 when the company relocated to 128 Babson St. (E19)

Occupied by Engine 46 temporarily from December 5, 1946 until June 26, 1947 when they returned to 1884 Dorchester Avenue.

Note: You will notice in the photo that this building has the appearance of one firehouse, but in reality it was two separate buildings with two separate patrol desks and no communication between the two.

9 GALLIVAN BOULEVARD

Built: December 31, 1958

Still in service. Engine 16 and District 8housed here.

Occupied by Engine 16 from December 31, 1958 until present.

Occupied by Ladder 6 from December 31, 1958 until January 14, 1982 when the company moved to 1884 Dorchester Avenue. (E18)

Occupied by District 8 from December 31, 1958 until present.

Occupied temporarily by Engine 52 from October 7, 1967 until October 18, 1967 when they returned to 120 Callender Street.

Occupied temporarily by Engine 24 from February 12, 1996 until June 13, 1996 while the firehouse at 36 Washington Street was being renovated.

One of the city's six one-story firehouses.

Another of Boston's one story firehouses, housing Engine 16 and District 8

MEETING HOUSE HILL

Built: Prior to January 3, 1870

Closed: June 27, 1927

Razed: New firehouse built on same site

Occupied by Dorchester Engine 2 prior to January 3, 1870 when the company was reorganized as Engine 17.

Occupied by Engine 17 from date of organization on January 3, 1870 until June 27, 1927 when the company moved to a temporary location on Parish Street while a new fire station was being constructed.

Occupied by Dorchester Ladder 2 prior to January 3, 1870 when company became Ladder 7.

Occupied by Ladder 7 from date of organization on January 3, 1870 until June 27, 1927 when the company moved to a temporary location on Parish Street while a new fire station was being constructed.

Occupied temporarily by Engine 21 Pump from July 18, 1925 until February 17, 1926 when the new firehouse was completed at 641 Columbia Road.

Parish Street, Dorchester

PARISH STREET (Temporary location)

Engine 17 located here from June 27, 1927 until February 15, 1928 when the company moved into the newly constructed firehouse at 7 Parish Street with Ladder 7 and District 10.

Ladder 7 located here from June 27, 1927 until February 15, 1928 when the company moved into the newly constructed firehouse at 7 Parish Street with Engine 17 and District 10.

7 PARISH STREET, MEETING HOUSE HILL

Built: February 15, 1928

Still in service, housing Engine 17, Ladder 7, and District 7.

Occupied by Engine 17 from February 15, 1928 until present.

Occupied by Ladder 7 from February 15, 1928 until present.

Occupied by District 10 from February 15, 1928 until May 4, 1954 when District 10 became District 7.

Occupied by District 7 from May 4, 1954 until present.

Note: The third floor was removed from the firehouse during renovations in 1950s.

As the firehouse was originally built in 1928

As it looks today with the third floor removed

30 HARVARD STREET

Built: Prior to January 3, 1870

Closed: June 11, 1960

Abandoned, still standing and used as a neighborhood civic facility

Occupied by Dorchester Engine 3 until January 3, 1870 when the company was reorganized as Engine 18.

Occupied by Engine 18 from date of organization on January 3, 1870 until September 21, 1954.

On September 21, 1954 Engine 18 became designated as Engine Squad 18.

Occupied by Engine Squad 18 from September 21, 1954 until June 11, 1960 when Engine Squad 18 relocated to 1884 Dorchester Avenue and this firehouse was abandoned.

Occupied by District 10 from date of organization on April 7, 1874 until February 15, 1928 when the district headquarters was relocated to a new firehouse at 7 Parish Street. (E17).

When the company was in service on Harvard Street

Notice that 'Engine 18' is still visible over the front doors

1884 DORCHESTER AVENUE

Built: October 5, 1894

Still in service, home to Engine 18 and Ladder 6.

Occupied by Combination Wagon 1 from date of reorganization on October 5, 1894 until January 10, 1907 when company was disbanded and reorganized as Chemical 11 and temporarily moved to a barn on Carlos Street.

Occupied by Engine 46 from date of organization on January 10, 1907 until December 5, 1946 when they were temporarily relocated to 51 River Street. (L6)

From June 4, 1917 until October 12, 1917 Engine 46 was temporarily located at 1867 Dorchester Avenue.

Occupied by Engine 46 from June 26, 1947 until August 12, 1958 when Engine 46 was disbanded.

Occupied by Engine 16 temporarily from August 12, 1958 until December 31, 1958 when they moved to a new firehouse at 9 Gallivan Boulevard.

Occupied by Engine Squad 18 from June 11, 1960 until July 1, 1969 when Engine Squad 18 was once again designated as Engine 18.

Occupied by Engine 18 from July 1, 1969 until June 26, 1995 when they moved temporarily to 301 Neponset Avenue. (E20)

Occupied by Engine 20 from December 20, 1995 until April 3, 2006 when they moved temporarily to 9 Gallivan Blvd. (E16)

Occupied by Engine 18 from August 21, 2006 until present.

Occupied by Ladder 27 from June 1, 1938 until November 25, 1946 when company was temporarily relocated to 32 Walnut Street. (E20)

Occupied by Ladder 27 from June 26, 1947 until they were relocated to a new fire station at 301 Neponset Avenue on August 12, 1958.

Occupied temporarily by Ladder 29 from October 7, 1967 until October 18, 1967 when they returned to 120 Callender Street.

Occupied by Ladder 6 from January 14, 1982 until June 26, 1995 when they were temporarily moved to 9 Gallivan Blvd. (E16)
Occupied by Ladder 6 from June 26, 1995 until April 3, 2006 when the company was temporarily moved to 301 Neponset Avenue. (E20)

Occupied by Ladder 6 from August 21, 2006 until present

Occupied by District 14 from date of organization on September 5, 1910 until May 4, 1954 when districts were reorganized with District 14 becoming District 8.

Occupied by District 8 from May 4, 1954 until Dec. 31, 1958 when the district headquarters was moved to a new firehouse at 9 Gallivan Boulevard. (E16)

Note: Original Combination Wagon 1 was organized at 4246 Washington Street, Roslindale and was in service from May 10, 1892 until September 17, 1894.

1884 Dorchester Avenue when only Engine 46 was quartered here

After the second door was added, as it looks today with Engine 18 and Ladder 6

128 BABSON STREET

(Original address was 786 Norfolk Street. Address changed on March 1, 1919 when this section of Norfolk Street became Babson Street)

Built: Prior to January 3, 1870

Closed: December 31, 1958

Abandoned and later razed. Vacant lot today

Occupied by Dorchester Engine 4 until January 3, 1870 when the company was reorganized as Engine 19.

Occupied by Engine 19 from date of organization on January 3, 1870 until December 31, 1958 when the company was disbanded and this firehouse was closed.

Occupied by Ladder 6 from June 1, 1938 until December 31, 1958 when they moved to a new firehouse at 9 Gallivan Boulevard (E16) and this firehouse was closed.

A grand old firehouse from the past

32 WALNUT STREET, PORT NORFOLK

Built: Prior to January 3, 1870

Closed: August 12, 1958

Abandoned and later razed - Today this is the site of a neighborhood park.

Occupied by Dorchester Engine 5 until January 3, 1870 when the company was reorganized as Engine 20.

Occupied by Engine 20 from date of organization on January 3, 1870 until August 12, 1958 when the company moved to a new firehouse at 301 Neponset Avenue and this firehouse was abandoned.

Occupied by Combination Ladder 11 from date of organization on November 15, 1901 until April 21, 1905 when the company was reorganized as Ladder 27.

Occupied by Ladder 27 from April 21, 1905 until June 1, 1938 when the company was relocated to 1884 Dorchester Avenue (E46).

Occupied temporarily by Ladder 27 from November 25, 1946 until June 26, 1947 when the company returned to 1884 Dorchester Avenue.

Today this site is a park

301 NEPONSET AVENUE

Built: August 12, 1958

Renovated: January 1999

Still in service, housing Engine 20.

Occupied by Engine 20 from August 12, 1958 until present.

Occupied by Ladder 27 from August 12, 1958 until July 15, 1977 when company was deactivated and reorganized as Aerial Tower 2.

Occupied by Aerial Tower 2 from July 15, 1977 until January 14, 1982 when Aerial Tower 2 was disbanded due to Proposition 2 ½.

Occupied by Safety Division Chief (H-1) from 1987 until June 20, 2001 when the Safety Division Chief moved to 174 Dudley Street. (E14)

Occupied by Engine 18 temporarily from June 26, 1995 until December 20, 1995 when they returned to 1884 Dorchester Avenue.

Occupied by Ladder 6 from April 3, 2006 until August 21, 2006 while their quarters were being remodeled.

Note: Firehouse underwent major renovations during 1999 during which time Engine 20 and H-1 occupied trailers on property.

301 Neponset Avenue was formerly occupied by Ladder 27 also

BOSTON STREET (now COLUMBIA ROAD)

Built: prior to January 3, 1870

Closed: July 18, 1925

Razed for new firehouse to be built on the same site

Occupied by Dorchester Engine 6 until January 3, 1870 when the company was reorganized as Engine 21.

Occupied by Engine 21 from date of organization on January 3, 1870 until July 18, 1925 when Engine 21 pump relocated to Engine 17 at 7 Parish Street and Engine 21 wagon to Engine 43 at 5 Boston Street while a new firehouse was being built on the same site.

As the first firehouse at this location originally looked

641 COLUMBIA ROAD

Built: February 17, 1926

Still in service, housing Engine 21.

Occupied by Engine 21 from February 17, 1926 until September 11, 1995 when they moved temporarily to 272 D Street. (E39)

Occupied by Engine 21 from January 27, 1996 until present.

Occupied by Lighting Plant 2 from December 16, 1974 until April 20, 1981 when it was placed out of service.

Occupied temporarily by the Rescue truck of the Rescue Pumper Unit from October 29, 1970 until November 6, 1970.

The second, and present day, firehouse at this location

As the firehouse looks today

36 WASHINGTON STREET, GROVE HALL

Built: November 8, 1898

Still in service with Engine 24 and Ladder 23 here.

Occupied by Combination Ladder 6 from the date of organization on November 8, 1898 until April 21, 1905 when the company was reorganized as Ladder 23.

Occupied by Ladder 23 from date of organization on April 21, 1905 until February 12, 1996 when they moved temporarily to 975 Blue Hill Avenue. (E52)

Occupied by Ladder 23 from June 13, 1996 until present.

Occupied by Division 3 from date of organization on September 14, 1913 until March 14, 1914 when division headquarters was moved to 198 Dudley Street. (L4)

Division 3 again relocated to 36 Washington Street from 198 Dudley Street (L4) on May 4, 1922 until February 4, 1947 when Divisions 2 and 3 were abolished.

The Boston Fire Department has two divisions again with Division 2 quartered here from January 5, 1949 until March 31, 1954 when the division headquarters was moved to 1870 Columbus Avenue. (E42)

Occupied temporarily by Engine 42 from August 6, 1926 until April 1, 1927 when they returned to their own quarters at 3089 Washington Street.

Temporarily occupied by Engine 24 from November 25, 1946 until March 27, 1947 when Engine 24 returned to its own quarters at 434 Warren Street.

Occupied by Lighting Plant 2 from date of service on November 4, 1947 until January 21, 1948 when it was moved to 618 Harrison Ave. (E3)

Occupied by Lighting Plant 3 from January 21, 1948 until May 1, 1956 when all Lighting Plants were placed in reserve.

Occupied by Engine 13 from June 11, 1960 until July 12, 1967 when Engine 13 was disbanded and reorganized as the Rescue-Pumper Unit.

Occupied by Rescue-Pumper Unit from July 12, 1967 until October 29, 1970 when temporarily, the pumper was relocated at 1870 Columbus Avenue (E42) and the rescue truck at 641 Columbia Road. (E21)

Occupied by the Rescue-Pumper Unit from November 6, 1970 until October 25, 1972 when the company was deactivated and reorganized as Rescue 2.

Occupied by Rescue 2 from date of reorganization on October 25, 1972 until August 16, 1973 when the company was relocated to 975 Blue Hill Avenue. (E52)

Occupied by Engine Company 24 from August 16, 1973 until February 12, 1996 when they were temporarily located at 9 Gallivan Blvd. (E16)

Occupied by Engine 24 from their return on June 13, 1996 until present.

36 Washington Street, Dorchester when the deputy was quartered here

And today.......

CARLOS STREET (barn)

Built: unknown

Closed: unknown

Very little is known about this building.

Occupied by Chemical 11 from January 10, 1907 until December 30, 1910 when the company moved to a new firehouse at 120 Callender Street.

120 CALLENDER STREET

Built: December 30, 1910

Closed: June 27, 1973

Building razed, site never developed

Occupied by Chemical 11 from December 30, 1910 until December 10, 1921 when the company was disbanded and reorganized as Engine 52.

Occupied by Engine 52 from date of organization on December 10, 1921 until October 7, 1967 when the company was temporarily relocated to 9 Gallivan Blvd.

Occupied by Engine 52 again from October 18, 1967 until June 27, 1973 when the company was relocated to a newly built firehouse at 975 Blue Hill Avenue.

Occupied by the first Combination City Service Ladder and Chemical Truck placed in service on December 19, 1912 and designated as Ladder 29. No company as yet organized.

Ladder Company 29 was organized on January 23, 1913 and occupied these quarters until October 7, 1967 when they were temporarily relocated to 1884 Dorchester Avenue. (E18)

Occupied by Ladder 29 from their return on October 18, 1967 until June 27, 1973 when the company was relocated to a new firehouse at 975 Blue Hill Avenue.

120 Callender Street, Dorchester former home of Engine 52 and Ladder 29

975 BLUE HILL AVENUE

Built: June 27, 1973

Still in service and occupied by Engine 52 and Ladder 29.

Occupied by Engine 52 from June 27, 1973 until present.

Occupied by Ladder 29 from June 27, 1973 until present.

Occupied by Rescue 2 from August 16, 1973 until April 10, 1981 when the company was relocated to 1870 Columbus Avenue, Roxbury. (E42)

Occupied temporarily by Ladder 23 from February 12, 1996 until June 13, 1996 when they returned to their own quarters at 36 Washington Street which had undergone renovations.

Rescue 2 was once an occupant here

LONG ISLAND

Built: April 10, 1946

Still in service

Occupied by Engine 54 from date of organization on April 10, 1946 until April 10, 1981 when the company was deactivated due to Proposition 2 ½.

Occupied by Ladder 33 from date of organization on April 10, 1946 until
October 14, 1957, when the company was renumbered as Ladder 31.

Occupied by Ladder 31 from October 14, 1957 until April 10, 1981 when the company was deactivated due to Proposition 2 ½.

Occupied by the Fire Brigade from date of organization on February 3, 1984, until present.

Note: Firehouse was closed from April 10, 1981 until February 3, 1984 when the Fire Brigade was organized and still occupies this firehouse until present. The Fire Brigade responds with a pumper and also has a 75 foot aerial ladder truck quartered with them.

Note: Bridge to Long Island opened on July 23, 1951. Prior to this date Long Island was only accessible by boat. Today traffic must pass through the city of Quincy to gain access Long Island and Moon Island.

A very simple building, not really designed as a firehouse

Today with second floor living area added

6

West Roxbury
Jamaica Plain
Roslindale

This annexation brought the Town of West Roxbury into the City of Boston. Today other neighborhoods have splintered from this area. There is Jamaica Plain, Roslindale and West Roxbury. All of these neighborhoods are predominantly residential although each has a business district.

Some of the finest neighborhoods in the city are found here. The tree-lined streets of Moss Hill in Jamaica Plain, Bellevue Hill in West Roxbury, and the Roslindale section abutting the Arnold Arboretum. The highest area in the city, sitting at 330 feet above sea level, is Bellevue Hill in West Roxbury.

Many nursing homes, a large hospital and a few commuter railroad stations can be found here. Jamaica Pond forms one of the borders between Jamaica Plain and the Town of Brookline. This large body of water is known for its fishing, boating and swimming.

The district also is the western border of the Turtle Pond Reservation. This is a large woodland area with many small ponds to be found here.

Richard Connelly

A winding, unlit roadway traverses this reservation so the companies are often called for auto accidents with entrapment.

Districts 10 and 12 cover this area in Division Two. Four firehouses in which there are four engines, three ladders, two District chiefs and the deputy of Division Two are located here.

659 CENTRE STREET

Built: 1872

Closed: December 18, 1984

Still standing and currently occupied as: J. P. Licks Ice Cream Shop

Occupied by Engine 28 from date of organization on January 5, 1874 when West Roxbury was annexed to the City of Boston until December 18, 1984 when the company moved to a new firehouse at 746 Centre Street.

Occupied by West Roxbury Ladder 1 until January 5, 1874 when the company was reorganized as Ladder 10.

Occupied by Ladder 10 from date of organization on January 5, 1874 until December 5, 1921 when the company was temporarily relocated to 16 Walk Hill Street with Chemical 13 until April 8, 1922.

Occupied by Ladder 10 from April 8, 1922 until May 25, 1954 when the company was again temporarily relocated to 16 Walk Hill Street with Engine 53 until April 27, 1955.

Occupied by Ladder 10 from April 27, 1955 until December 18, 1984 when the company moved to a new firehouse at 746 Centre Street.

Occupied by District 12 from date of organization on August 1, 1912 until May 4, 1954 when districts were reorganized and District 12 was renumbered as District 9.

Occupied by District 9 from May 4, 1954 until December 18, 1984 when the district headquarters were relocated to 1870 Columbus Avenue (E 42).

659 Centre Street in the 1950s

Today this ice cream shop occupies the old Jamaica Plain firehouse

746 CENTRE STREET

Built: December 18, 1984

Still in service, housing Engine 28, Tower Ladder 10 and the Deputy of Division 2.

Occupied by Engine 28 from December 18, 1984 until present.

Occupied by Ladder 10 from December 18, 1984 until May 30, 2002 when Ladder 10 became designated as Tower Ladder 10.

Occupied by Tower Ladder 10 from May 30, 2002 until present.

Occupied by Division 2 from December 18, 1984 until present.

Note: When Tower Ladder companies are running with a spare ladder truck, the company designation on the department radio is "Ladder". This signifies that the tower ladder is out of service and reminds the incident commander that there is no tower arriving when he/she is expecting it.

The Jamaica Plain firehouse today

MOUNT VERNON STREET near CENTRE STREET

Built: prior to 1876

Closed: June 1, 1898

Building razed

Occupied by a hand engine company from an unknown date until September 21, 1876 when it was replaced by Chemical 7.

Occupied by Chemical 7 from date of organization on September 21, 1876 until July 10, 1883 when the company was disbanded.

Occupied by Engine 30 from date of organization on July 10, 1883 until June 1, 1898 when the company moved to a new firehouse at 1940 Centre Street.

1940 CENTRE STREET

Built: June 1, 1898

Still in service housing Engine 30 and Ladder 25.

Occupied by Engine 30 from June 1, 1898 until April 1996 when they were temporarily relocated to 5115 Washington Street. (E55) while their quarters were being remodeled.

Occupied by Engine 30 from August 23, 1996 until present.

Occupied by Combination Ladder 9 from date of organization on April 23, 1900 until April 21, 1905 when the company became Ladder 25.

Occupied by Ladder 25 from date of organization on April 21, 1905 until April 1996 when they moved temporarily to 5115 Washington Street. (E55)

Occupied by Ladder 25 from June 1996 until September 1, 2005 when they again temporarily moved to 5115 Washington Street (E55)

Occupied by Ladder 25 from January 18, 2006 until present.

Engine 30 and Ladder 25

Although 90 years old, this firehouse hasn't really changed much

16 WALKHILL STREET

Built: July 29, 1910

Closed: June 11, 1959

Presently used as an apartment house.

Occupied by Chemical 13 from date of organization on July 29, 1910 until December 10, 1921 when the company was disbanded.

Occupied by Engine 53 from date of organization on December 10, 1921 until September 21, 1954 when the company designation was changed to Engine Squad 53.

Occupied by Ladder 10 temporarily from December 5, 1921 until April 8, 1922 when they returned to 659 Centre Street.

Occupied by Ladder 10 temporarily from May 25, 1954 until April 27, 1955 when they again returned to 659 Centre Street.

Occupied by Engine Squad 53 from September 21, 1954 until April 4, 1956 when Engine 45 moved from 4246 Washington St. to 16 Walk Hill St. and was designated as Engine 53. Engine Squad 53 moved to 4246 Washington St. and was designated as Engine Squad 45.

Occupied by Engine 53 from April 4, 1956 until June 11, 1959 when the company moved to a new firehouse at 315 Cummins Highway.

Engine 53 on Walkhill Street in days gone by

The firehouse still stands today and is home to some civilian families

4246 WASHINGTON STREET in Roslindale Square

Built: January 20, 1875

Closed: June 11, 1959

Building razed and a Boston Public Library occupies the site today.

Occupied by Chemical 4 from date of organization on January 20, 1875 until March 10, 1892 when the company was disbanded.

Occupied by Combination Wagon 1 from date of organization on March 10, 1892 until September 17, 1894 when the company was disbanded.

Occupied by Engine 45 from date of organization on September 17, 1894 until April 4, 1956 when the company moved to 16 Walkhill Street and renumbered as Engine 53. Engine Squad 53 moved to 4246 Washington Street and was designated Engine Squad 45.

Occupied by Engine Squad 45 from April 4, 1956 until June 11, 1959 when they moved to a new firehouse at 315 Cummins Highway.

Occupied by Ladder 16 from date of organization on October 12, 1888 until June 11, 1959 when they moved to a new firehouse at 315 Cummins Highway.

Occupied by District 13 from date of organization on March 14, 1914 until May 4, 1954 when District 13 became District 10 due to redistricting.

Occupied by District 10 from May 4, 1954 until June 11, 1959 when they moved to a new firehouse at 315 Cummings Highway. (E53)

The Roslindale Square firehouse in the way back

A grand old firehouse torn down to make way for a library

The Roslindale Branch of the Boston Public Library sits on the old firehouse site today

315 CUMMINS HIGHWAY (original address)

945 CANTERBURY STREET (As of Nov. 21, 1961)

Built: June 11, 1959

Still in service

Occupied by Engine Squad 45 from June 11, 1959 until July 31, 1969 when the company designation was changed back to Engine 45.

Occupied by Engine 45 from July 31, 1969 until April 10, 1981 when Engine 45 was deactivated due to Proposition 2 ½.

Occupied by Engine 53 from June 11, 1959 until present.

Occupied by Ladder 16 from June 11, 1959 until present.

Occupied by District 10 until June 29, 1971 when they relocated to 5115 Washington Street (E55) due to redistricting.

Occupied by newly established District 12 from June 29, 1971 until present.

Occupied by Haz-Mat Unit (H3) from July 1, 1997 until November 1, 2001 when it was relocated to 700 Tremont Street. (E22)

One of only six single story firehouses

5115 WASHINGTON STREET

Built: June 6, 1949

Remodeled: 1976

Still in service

Occupied by Engine 55 from date of organization on June 6, 1949 until present.

Occupied by newly reorganized Ladder 5 from date of reactivation on January 8, 1975 until the company was deactivated on April 10, 1981 due to Proposition 2 ½.

Occupied by District 10 from June 29, 1971 until present.

Occupied by Brush Unit 55 which responds with Engine 55 when needed.

Temporarily occupied by Ladder 25 from April 1996 for a few months and again from September 1, 2005 until January 18, 2006.

Note: Firehouse remodeled January 8, 1975 by moving front wall closer to street so that a tiller ladder truck could fit.

This photo shows how Engine 55's firehouse looked when built

5115 Washington Street as it looks today

7

Charlestown

The Charlestown section of the city is also separated from the mainland by water. Boston Harbor and the Charles River are the waterways.

History buffs may recognize that the Bunker Hill Monument is situated here on, where else but, Bunker Hill. Bunker Hill is also known to locals as Breeds Hill. It is the site of a 221 foot granite block monument. There are 294 steps, if you wish to climb to the top for a spectacular view of the city and the harbor.

The former Charlestown navy yard is located here as well as the most famous warship of the U. S. Navy, the USS Constitution. The condominiums located in the old navy yard have a fantastic water view and a 15 minute walk to downtown Boston. There is also a marina here, something that you usually don't find under a city's skyline.

The Tobin Bridge, a double decked commuter toll bridge, brings traffic into the city from the north. This bridge has its southern terminus in Charlestown.

Once again, this predominantly residential neighborhood has three-deckers, row houses, and quite a few brick tenements. This section of the city has two firehouses today, housing two engines and one ladder company. It is in Fire District 3, which is in Division One.

326 MAIN STREET

Built: Prior to January 5, 1874 when Charlestown was annexed to Boston

Closed: October 20, 1885 – Building razed. Public housing now exists on this site.

Occupied by Ladder 9 from date of Charlestown's annexation to the city of Boston on January 5, 1874 until October 20, 1885 when the company relocated to new quarters at 333 Main Street.

Occupied by Hose 1 from the date of annexation on January 5, 1874 until October 20, 1885 when the company moved to new quarters at 333 Main Street.

Predecessor of Ladder 9

556 MAIN STREET

Built: Prior to January 5, 1874 when Charlestown was annexed to Boston

Closed: March 17, 1884 – Building razed. This area today is a roadway.

Occupied by Hose 2 from before the annexation on January 5, 1874 until March 17, 1884 when the company was disbanded and this firehouse was abandoned.

Bunker Hill Day (June 17th) apparently

34 WINTHROP STREET

Built: 1874

Still in service

Occupied by Hose 3 from January 5, 1874 when Charlestown was annexed to Boston until December 24, 1894 when the company was relocated to 44 Monument Street.

Occupied temporarily by Chemical 9 from December 24, 1894 until May 20, 1895.

Occupied again by Hose 3 from May 20, 1895 until May 4, 1898 when the company was disbanded.

Occupied by Combination Wagon 7 from the date of organization on May 4, 1898 until April 21, 1905 when the company was re-designated as Combination Wagon 2.

Occupied by Combination Wagon 2 from the date of organization on April 21, 1905 until January 10, 1907 when the company was re-designated Chemical Engine 3.

Occupied by Chemical Engine 3 from January 10, 1907 until November 30, 1917 when the company was disbanded.

Occupied by Engine 50 from date of organization on July 26, 1918 until April 10, 1981 when the company was disbanded due to Proposition 2 ½.

Engine 50 reactivated on May 9, 1981 and has remained in service at this location until present.

Occupied by District 2 from July 26, 1918 until April 10, 1981 when District 2 was disbanded. The district and fire companies were absorbed into District 3.

Occupied temporarily by Rescue 3 when the company was organized on May 31, 1929 until November 14, 1930 when Rescue 3 moved to Bowdoin Sq.

This is the second oldest firehouse in the City of Boston

BUNKER HILL AND TUFTS STREETS

Built: Prior to January 5, 1874 when Charlestown was annexed to Boston

Closed: October 20, 1885 – Building razed

Occupied by Hose 4 from sometime prior to January 5, 1874 when Charlestown was annexed to Boston until October 20, 1885 when the company moved to a new firehouse at 44 Monument Street and the old firehouse was abandoned.

44 MONUMENT STREET

Built: October 20, 1885

Closed: November 13, 1972 – Abandoned by the city. Building heavily damaged by fire on November 23, 1973 and again on September 24, 1974 – Building razed after the second fire. This firehouse was unique since a public housing development was built around it.

Occupied by Hose 4 from October 20, 1885 until September 16, 1890 when Hose 4 become designated as Engine 36.

Occupied by Engine 36 from September 16, 1890 until November 13, 1972 when the company moved to 525 Main Street.

Occupied by Combination Ladder 5 from date of organization on February 11, 1898 until April 21, 1905 when the company was designated as Ladder 22.

Occupied by Ladder 22 from April 21, 1905 until November 13, 1972 when Ladder 22 was relocated to the quarters of Engine 51 in Brighton at 425 Faneuil Street.

Notice that everything around the firehouse was leveled when the public housing development was constructed

11 ELM STREET

Built: unknown

Closed: April 22, 1938 – Building razed, remains a vacant lot.

Occupied by Engine 27 when Charlestown was annexed to Boston on January 5, 1874 until December 24, 1894 when the company moved temporarily to 333 Main Street. (L9)

Occupied by Engine 27 from May 20, 1895 until April 22, 1938 when they moved to 333 Main Street. (L9) and this firehouse was abandoned and later razed.

This former firehouse site is another vacant lot today

Richard Connelly

333 MAIN STREET

Built: October 20, 1885

Closed: July 1, 1961 – Building razed, vacant lot today

Occupied by Hose 1 from October 20, 1885 until July 17, 1888 when the company was disbanded.

Occupied by Chemical Engine 9 from date of organization on July 17, 1888 until December 24, 1894 when the company was temporarily relocated to 34 Winthrop Street, (E50)

Occupied by Chemical 9 from May 20, 1895 until July 26, 1918 when the company was disbanded.

Occupied by Ladder 9 from October 20, 1885 until July 1, 1961 when the company moved to 440 Bunker Hill Street.

Occupied temporarily by Engine 27 from December 24, 1894 until May 20, 1895 when they returned to 11 Elm Street.

Occupied by Engine 27 from April 22, 1938 until July 1, 1961 when Engine 27 was disbanded.

Occupied by District 2 from date of organization on April 7, 1874 until July 26, 1918 when the district headquarters was moved to 34 Winthrop Street. (E50).

Another of Boston's firehouses under the elevated structure at 333 Main Street

440 BUNKER HILL STREET

Built: March 17, 1884

Closed: October 16, 1970 – Presently used as: Dance Workshop

Occupied by Engine 32 from the date of organization on March 17, 1884 until October 16, 1970 when they moved to a new firehouse at 525 Main Street.

Occupied by Ladder 9 from July 1, 1961 until October 16, 1970 when they moved to a new firehouse at 525 Main Street.

Engine 32 and Ladder 9 on Bunker Hill Street

The old firehouse as it stands today occupied by a dance studio

525 MAIN STREET

Built: October 16, 1970

Still in service

Occupied by Engine 32 from October 16, 1970 until present.

Occupied by Engine 36 from November 13, 1972 until October 20, 1981 when the company was disbanded due to Proposition 2 ½.

Occupied by Ladder 9 from October 16, 1970 until present.

This firehouse also housed Engine 36 when it was built

8

Brighton

The Brighton section of the city also contains the area known as Allston. Allston is the lower area closest to the city proper. The town of Brighton was annexed to the City of Boston on January 5, 1874. Many apartment buildings occupy the area and are home to students of Boston University and Boston College as well as the working class. A substantial portion of the private dwellings in this area have been converted into apartments for students disregarding their original usage as single-family homes. The population is quite higher during the school year than in the summer.

A fair share of the area is now owned by Harvard University and construction is running rampant in the areas nearest to the city of Cambridge.

Brighton has a myriad of apartment buildings lining Commonwealth Avenue and the streets running off of Commonwealth Avenue. As you approach the city line just before the city of Newton, both single family and two-family homes abound. There are quite a few three-deckers as well. Brighton also has its share of industrial and office building occupancies.

The Massachusetts Turnpike slices through the area and there are numerous streetcar lines plus a substantial railroad yard.

The Brighton district has three firehouses housing three engines and two ladders with a district chief.

20 CHESTNUT HILL AVENUE

Built: Prior to January 5, 1874 when Brighton was annexed to Boston.

Closed: December 20, 1929

Presently used as a neighborhood services center.

Occupied by Engine 29 from prior to January 5, 1874 until December 20, 1929 when the company was relocated to 138 Chestnut Hill Avenue.

Occupied by Ladder 11 from prior to January 5, 1874 until December 20, 1929 when the company was relocated to 138 Chestnut Hill Avenue.

One block from Brighton Center. (Washington Street and Chestnut Hill Avenue)

The building has been modernized, but you can still picture it as a firehouse

138 CHESTNUT HILL AVENUE

Built: December 29, 1929

Still in service.

Occupied by Engine 29 from December 20, 1929 until April 6, 1956 when Engine 29 exchanged quarters with Engine Squad 34. Engine 29 became designated as Engine Squad 29 and Engine Squad 34 became designated as Engine 34.

Occupied by Engine Squad 29 from April 6, 1956 until July 31, 1969 when Engine Squad 29 was again designated as Engine 29.

Occupied as Engine 29 from July 31, 1969 until present.

Occupied by Ladder 11 from December 20, 1929 until present.

Occupied by District 11 from July 7, 1959 until present.

Engine 29, Ladder 11, District 11 today

444 WESTERN AVENUE

Built: November 3, 1888

Closed: April 10, 1981

Building presently used as an office building.

Occupied by Engine 34 from November 3, 1888 until September 21, 1954 when Engine 34 was designated as Engine Squad 34.

Occupied by Engine Squad 34 from September 21, 1954 until April 6, 1956 when Engine Squad 34 once again became designated as Engine 34.

Occupied by Engine 34 until company was disbanded on April 10, 1981 due to Proposition 2 ½.

Note: On April 6, 1956 Engine Squad 34 and Engine 29 exchanged quarters and company designations with Engine Squad 34 becoming Engine Squad 29 and Engine 29 becoming Engine 34.

Another grand old firehouse

Remarkably the firehouse hasn't changed much in the 27 years it has been closed

16 HARVARD AVENUE near CAMBRIDGE STREET

Built: Prior to May 1, 1876

Closed: 1889

Building razed for a new firehouse to be built on the same site.

Occupied by Chemical Engine 6 from date of organization on May 1, 1876 until December 22, 1890 when the company relocated to new quarters at 16 Harvard Avenue.

16 HARVARD AVENUE

Built: December 22, 1890   (second firehouse on this site)

Closed: June 15, 1977

Firehouse has been recently used as an antique shop, music shop, and office space.

Occupied by Chemical Engine 6 from December 22, 1890 until April 23, 1915 when the company was disbanded

Occupied by Engine 41 from February 10, 1893 until June 15, 1977 when the company moved to a new firehouse at 460 Cambridge Street.

Occupied by Ladder 14 from date of reorganization on April 5, 1916 until June 15, 1977 when the company moved to a new firehouse at 460 Cambridge Street in Union Square.

Occupied by District 11 until July 7, 1959 when District 11 was relocated to 138 Chestnut Hill Avenue. (E29)

The firehouse was originally built with only one door

A second door was added for Ladder 14

16 Harvard Avenue as it looks today

460 CAMBRIDGE STREET

Built: June 15, 1977

Still in service.

Occupied by Engine 41 from June 15, 1977 until present.

Occupied by Ladder 14 from June 15, 1977 until present.

Note: This firehouse was built with the intention of relocating Engine 34 here, but it never came to fruition due to neighborhood activists and Engine 34 remained at 444 Western Avenue.

This firehouse is in Union Square, Allston and is just two blocks from the old house

425 FANEUIL STREET

Built: February 24, 1913.

Still in service.

Occupied by Ladder 31 from February 24, 1913 until July 12, 1920 when the company was disbanded.

Occupied by Engine 51 from date of organization on July 12, 1920 until present..

Occupied by Ladder 34 from date of organization on March 15, 1950 until May 25, 1954 when the company was disbanded.

Occupied by Ladder 22 from November 13, 1972 until April 10, 1981 when the company was disbanded due to Proposition 2 ½.

Richard Connelly

Ladder 31, Ladder 34, and Ladder 22 have all been in this firehouse

9

Hyde Park

The last community to be annexed to the City of Boston was the Town of Hyde Park. With the annexation came two fire stations with two engine companies and two ladder companies.

Hyde Park is extremely residential with the exception of businesses along Hyde Park Avenue and River Street. The western edge of Hyde Park is quite forested. Three railroad lines run through the center of the district. The New York, New Haven and Hartford Railroad once had an enormous storage yard and repair facility here.

The Stop and Shop supermarket chain had one of the largest buildings in the city in the Readville section of Hyde Park. This warehouse supplied the entire Stop and Shop supermarket chain. It has since moved from Readville, but remains in Massachusetts.

The streets of the Fairmount Hill section of Hyde Park are lined with Victorian, Georgian, and Queen Anne style homes. The Boston Police Department has their police academy in the Fairmount Hill section of Hyde Park.

The Cleary Square area is the focus of the business district and has a fromer opera house, church, public library and scores of small storefront businesses lining Hyde Park Avenue, River Street and Fairmount Avenue.

Today, there are two firehouses housing two engine companies and one ladder company.

HYDE PARK CENTRAL FIRE STATION

Built: unknown

Closed: Circa 1912

Little is known about this fire house. Apparently it was the predecessor of the Winthrop Street firehouse.

Town of Hyde Park Central firehouse

30 WINTHROP STREET corner HARVARD AVENUE

Built: 1910

Closed: December 14, 1972

Abandoned and later destroyed by fire. (Two alarms on box 3741 on November 27, 1976) – Remains a vacant lot today.

Occupied by Hose 48 from January 1, 1912 when Hyde Park annexed to City of Boston until February 2, 1912.

Occupied by Engine 48, which was organized to replace Hose 48, on February 2, 1912 until December 14, 1972 when the company moved to a newly constructed fire station at 60 Fairmount Avenue.

Occupied by Hyde Park Ladder 1 until January 1, 1912 when Hyde Park annexed to City of Boston.

Occupied by Ladder 28 from date of reorganization on January 1, 1912 until December 14, 1972 when the company moved to a newly constructed firehouse at
60 Fairmount Avenue.

Occupied by Chemical 14 from January 1, 1912 until June 23, 1920 when company disbanded.

Occupied by District 15 from January 1, 1912 until May 4, 1954 when districts were reorganized and District 15 was abolished.

This old firehouse was destroyed by fire on November22, 1976 (2-3741)

60 FAIRMOUNT AVENUE

Built: December 14, 1972

Still in service

Occupied by Engine 48 from December 14, 1972 until present.

Occupied by Ladder 28 from December 14, 1972 until present.

Occupied by Brush Unit 48 which responds with Engine 48 when needed.

Note: Originally intended for Engine 49 to move to this fire house, however neighborhood activists were successful in keeping Engine 49 in their own quarters at 209 Neponset Valley Parkway.

Engine 48's house at 60 Fairmount Avenue has a large basement area for the storage of unused apparatus with entry in the rear

WEST MILTON ST. opp. READVILLE ST.

Built: prior to January 1, 1912

Closed: July 26, 1918 – Building razed

Occupied by Hose 49 from prior to January 1, 1912 until July 26, 1918 when the company was disbanded and reorganized as Engine 49 at the corner of Milton and Hamilton Streets in a newly built firehouse.

The old term 'firebarn' is certainly fitting here

209 NEPONSET VALLEY PARKWAY

(Originally named Milton Street)

Built: July 26, 1918

Still in service

Occupied by Engine 49 from date of organization on July 26, 1918 until January 14, 1981 when company was disbanded.

Occupied by Engine 49 again when the company was reestablished on July 21, 1982 until present.

Occupied by Ladder 32 from date of organization on February 20, 1946 until the company was deactivated on May 25, 1954.

Note: On January 31, 1934 the address of the firehouse was changed to 209 Neponset Valley Parkway.

Three blocks from the town of Milton, five blocks from the town of Dedham

10

Administrative Division

FIRE HEADQUARTERS

CITY HALL, SCHOOL STREET, Downtown

Built: 1865

Moved: May 6, 1890

Building still standing, used as an office building, restaurant, etc.

Old City Hall in Boston, site of the first Fire Headquarters

94 TREMONT STREET, Downtown

Leased quarters: May 6, 1890

Moved: July 1, 1895

Moved from this location to the newly built fire headquarters at 60 Bristol Street.

60 BRISTOL STREET, South End

Built: July 1, 1895

Closed: August 6, 1951

Still standing - Presently occupied by the Pine Street Inn, a homeless shelter

Fire Headquarters moved to the newly built building at 115 Southampton Street.

60 Bristol Street, which was the first Fire Headquarters in its own dedicated building

115 SOUTHAMPTON STREET, Roxbury

Built: August 6, 1951

Still in service

This building is part of a complex that houses Fire Headquarters, Repair Shops, and a firehouse. Due to a lack of space, recently the Fire Prevention Division moved its operation to leased space in an office building at 1010 Massachusetts Avenue, three blocks from HQ.

This location is still in service with other outside space leased also

FIRE ALARM OFFICE

At 12 noon on April 28, 1852 the fire alarm telegraph system of the Boston Fire Department entered into service. This was the first fire alarm system in the world. Dr. William F. Channing and Professor Moses G. Farmer were the inventors of this fire alarm telegraph system.

COURT SQUARE and WILLIAMS COURT, Downtown

Opened: April 28, 1852

Closed: December 26, 1865 - No further information

CITY HALL, Downtown Boston

Opened: December 26, 1895

Moved: May 20, 1895

Building still standing and is currently used as office space, a restaurant, and other occupancies.

60 BRISTOL STREET, South End

Built: May 20, 1895

Closed: December 27, 1925

Building still standing (see photo page 221)

59 THE FENWAY, Back Bay

Built: December 27, 1925

Still in service

When this location began operations, the alarm transmitter equipment in use had been in service since 1893. These transmitters were used into the 1970s. New equipment has been introduced twice in the last 30 years. Today a modern, computer aided system is in service.

Two-way radios were installed in all department vehicles by June 7, 1954.

Currently, the city's 911 center is at Boston Police Headquarters at Shroeder Plaza in Roxbury. Call takers answer calls for Police and EMS, but the fire calls are transferred to the Fire Alarm Office.

This location has seen extensive remodeling in the last few years. The city's backup 911 center occupies the basement area of the Fire Alarm Office at 59 The Fenway.

This fortress style building houses the BFD's Fire Alarm Office

DEPARTMENT SHOPS

BRISTOL STREET, South End

Built: April 1, 1875

Destroyed by fire: August 9, 1910

363 ALBANY STREET at Bristol Street, South End

Built: July 11, 1911

Closed: August 6, 1951

Building still standing, commercial use

This building at 363 Albany Street is still standing and once housed the department shops

900 MASSACHUSETTS AVENUE

Built: August 6, 1951

Still in service

Today this complex houses the shops, headquarters and, at one time, a firehouse

DEPARTMENT DRILL SCHOOL

60 BRISTOL STREET, South End

Built: 1889

Closed: August 6, 1951

In the interim between 1951 and 1960 the old U. S. Navy fire school in South Boston was used.

MOON ISLAND FIRE ACADEMY

Built: November 30, 1960

Still in service

Dedicated as the Chief John A. Martin Fire Academy

Newly built state of the art burn building opened on July 28, 2008.

This is the present day fire academy on Moon Island

The BFD's new burn building, dedicated in 2008

HIGH PRESSURE STATIONS

Boston has a separate set of high pressure mains running throughout the downtown area. These mains pump water by using a pumping station which is activated when box alarms are struck downtown. Although the system is ancient, it still works today.

Hydrants for this system can be identified by the four 2 ½" outlets and the red bonnet.

HIGH PRESSURE STATION 1

Lincoln Power Station (Boston Elevated Railway)
Commercial and Battery Streets

Opened: January 23, 1922

Closed: December 14, 1931

HIGH PRESSURE STATION 1
165 KNEELAND STREET

Built: December 14, 1931

Closed: December 25, 1981

Building razed

HIGH PRESSURE STATION 1
175 KNEELAND STREET

Built: December 25, 1981

Still in service

A newly built High Pressure Station remotely operated from the Fire Alarm Office.

HIGH PRESSURE STATION 2

Boston Edison Station
Atlantic Avenue & Pearl Street

Opened: December 19, 1921

Closed: December 25, 1981

Building razed – Hotel built on former site

11

Marine Division

The City of Boston has many miles of waterfront. Fireboats have always been a mainstay of fire protection for the property along the Atlantic Ocean. Marine companies have been stationed in fire houses, on the boats themselves and now their quarters are in a condominium complex with the Marine Unit occupying a first floor unit next to their dock.

There is nothing as spectacular as seeing the fireboat in action at a multiple alarm blaze with four or five guns being played on the fire.

The Marine unit today works in conjunction with the Boston Fire Department Dive Team. At many incidents, the fireboat is the base for operations so that the divers work safely and efficiently.

This section lists all of the berths that fireboats and the Marine unit occupied from the first in 1912 to today's quarters on burroughs Wharf.

CENTRAL WHARF

Abandoned: October 29, 1912

On January 1, 1873, the "William M. Flanders" was the first fireboat to be placed in service. It had no company number originally. In March 1881 the "William M. Flanders" moved to India Wharf.

On September 14, 1898 Engine 31 was placed in service again, as a reserve boat.

Engine 44 relocated here sometime during 1905 until October 29, 1912 when they moved to a new berth at the Northern Avenue Bridge.

INDIA WHARF

Abandoned: 1906

In March, 1881 the "William M. Flanders" was moved to this location.

On January 17, 1884 the "William M. Flanders" was designated as Engine Company 31 until deactivated on September 1, 1895.

On September 1, 1895 Engine 44 was organized with a new fireboat at India Wharf until May 5, 1907 when Engine 44 moved to Central Wharf.

FOOT of LEWIS STREET, EAST BOSTON

Abandoned: March 10, 1948

August, 1909 saw Engine 47 organized with a new fireboat and remained here until some time in 1943 when Engine 47 was put out of service. The Boat remained here until Engine 47 was again placed in service on March 10, 1948 at which time the company was moved to the foot of Battery Street.

Marine District 13 established and quartered here on October 14, 1909.
District 13 abolished on February 6, 1914.

On March 15, 1911 Engine 31 was placed back into active service and located here until August 5, 1911 when they moved to a new firehouse at 521 Commercial Street.

Engine 31 again located here temporarily from January 15, 1919 until May 7, 1924 when they returned to 521 Commercial Street after their quarters were rebuilt.

521 COMMERCIAL STREET

Abandoned: March 24, 1954

Occupied by Engine 31 from August 5, 1911 until January 15, 1919 when their quarters were destroyed in the Molasses Disaster.

Temporarily occupied by Engine 8 from October 30, 1916 until July 5, 1917

Firehouse wrecked during Molasses Disaster on January 15, 1919. One member killed when he drowned in molasses while trapped under debris.

Firehouse rebuilt and Engine 31 returned on May 7, 1924 until October 22, 1948 when they moved to the foot of Battery Street.

Also on October 22, 1948, Engine 44 moved into Engine 31's old berth at this location until March 24, 1954 when Engine 44's assignments were cancelled.

NORTHERN AVENUE BRIDGE

Abandoned: October 22, 1948

The firehouse here was occupied by the members of Engine 44 from October 29, 1912 when Engine 44 moved here from Central Wharf and remained at this location until October 22, 1948 when they moved to 521 Commercial Street.

Engine 44's firehouse at the Northern Avenue Bridge

FOOT OF BATTERY STREET (BATTERY WHARF)

Engine 31 berthed here from October 22, 1948 until October 12, 1950 when they were relocated to Castle Island terminal.

Engine 31 berthed here again from November 29, 1950 until September 12, 1969 when they moved to Lincoln Wharf.

Engine 31 returned to Battery Wharf on July 13, 1972.

Engine 47 berthed here from March 10, 1948 until September 12, 1969 when they too moved to Lincoln Wharf.

Engine 47 returned to Battery Wharf on July 13, 1972.

On September 15, 1976 Engine 31 and Engine 47 were disbanded and the Marine Unit was placed in service. The Marine Unit now consists of two vessels, Marine Unit 1 and Marine Unit 2. The Marine Unit remained here until July 14, 1988 when the company was temporarily relocated to Pier 4 in Charlestown.

CASTLE ISLAND TERMINAL

Abandoned: November 29, 1950

Engine 31 moved here on October 12, 1950, but returned to Battery Wharf on November 29, 1950.

LINCOLN WHARF

Abandoned: July 13, 1972

Engine 31 temporarily moved here from September 12, 1969 until July 13, 1972 when they relocated to Battery Wharf.

Engine 47 temporarily moved here from September 12, 1969 until July 13, 1972 when they relocated to Battery Wharf.

PIER 4, CHARLESTOWN

Abandoned: May 16, 1991

On July 14, 1988 the Marine Unit moved here until new quarters were completed on May 16, 1991.

BURROUGHS WHARF

On May 16, 1991 the Marine Unit returned from Pier 4 to new quarters at the end of Burroughs Wharf. (Formerly Battery Wharf)

The Marine Unit occupies this floor condo as its firehouse

Firemen's Memorial Lot

This beautiful bronze 26 foot high statue mounted on a granite base was erected in 1909. It was originally intended as the burial place of indigent firefighters under the auspices of the Charitable Association of the Boston Fire Department. This rule has since been rescinded.

The second Sunday in June is Memorial Sunday in the Boston Fire Department as it is in many other departments. Each year the Charitable Association holds a memorial service beginning with a Catholic Mass in the chapel of the Forest Hills Cemetery in the Jamaica Plain section of the city. The participants then march up to the gravesite guarded by this honorable monument. The president of the Charitable Association, the Fire Commissioner, the Chief of Department and a guest orator make brief comments which are followed by a prayer from either the Catholic, Jewish or Protestant Chaplain on a rotating schedule. The graves are then decorated with flowers and the Gaelic Brigade pipe band plays a musical piece.

Firemen's Memorial lot in Forest Hills Cemetery

GLOSSARY

For those of you who are not familiar with Boston's history and for those of you who are not familiar with fire service jargon this is an attempt to acquaint you with some of the language and terms found in this book.

<u>Aide</u>: Deputy Fire Chiefs (Division Chiefs) have available to them, an Aide who is usually a senior, experienced firefighter. Most Deputy Chiefs retain the ICT that they chose when they were a DFC.

<u>Box Alarm</u>: When a box alarm is transmitted over the fire alarm tappers and bells, it is in response to a verbal report of a building fire or a similar emergency which is determined to require a large number of personnel.
Three engines, two ladders, one rescue company and a District Chief respond. In some areas, a Deputy Chief, the Marine Unit and/or a Tower Ladder may also respond.

<u>District</u>: A district is a section of the city commanded by a District Fire Chief (DFC), known in some cities as a Battalion Chief. The DFC may have from 4 to 8 companies in the district.

<u>Division</u>: The city is divided into two divisions. The boundary is basically divided by Massachusetts Avenue. The north side of Massachusetts Avenue is Division One and the south side is Division Two with the exception of the Brighton/Allston district (District 11),

which geographically lies south of Massachusetts Avenue, but is in Division One.

Fire Brigade: Engine 54 and Ladder 31 on Long Island were disbanded in 1981. After the dust settled from Proposition 2 ½ the Fire Brigade was established at the Long Island Hospital Shelter for fire protection.

Incident Command Technicians (ICT): District Fire Chiefs have an ICT available to him/her to perform duties such as driving, sizing up, reporting to, and keeping track of the location of companies assigned to an alarm. This ICT is chosen by the DFC and is usually an experienced senior member of the BFD. This is an extremely important position in the BFD. Formerly known as an aide.

Marine Unit: In 1972 Engines 31 and 47, which were fireboats, were deactivated and became known as the Marine Unit. This company responded with two boats, Marine Unit 1 and Marine Unit 2.

MetroFire (Fire District 13): The Commonwealth of Massachusetts is separated into fire districts in which the various fire departments operate in cooperation with each other, supplying necessary apparatus and personnel when a major emergency occurs. The Metro Fire District is comprised of 35 cities or towns. They are: Arlington, Belmont, Boston, Braintree, Brookline, Burlington, Cambridge, Chelsea, Dedham, Everett, Lexington, Lynn, Malden, Massport, Medford, Melrose, Milton, Needham, Newton, Quincy, Randolph, Reading, Revere, Saugus, Somerville, Stoneham, Wakefield, Waltham, Watertown, Wellesley, Weston, Weymouth, Winchester, Winthrop, and Woburn.

Minimum strength: The minimum strength is 1 officer and three firefighters per tour assigned to any company. A senior firefighter may temporarily replace the officer for vacations, sick tours or injured leave.

Proposition 2 ½: Under the mayoral administration of Kevin H. White property taxes were to be held to a maximum of 2 ½ percent of the assessed value. Although this was an edict in the entire Commonwealth of Massachusetts, it had particularly strong implications in the City of Boston.

22 fire companies were disbanded with only three ever opening again. Two fire houses were permanently closed.

The following companies were disbanded:

Engines 1, 11, 12, 25, 26, 34, 36, 40, 43, 45, 49, 50, 54

Ladders 5, 8, 13, 20, 22, 27, 30, 31

Rescue 2

Engine 34 and Engine 43's houses were both closed.

Through efforts of the community, the city was never completely successful in closing Engines 49 and 50. Rescue 2 was reactivated on June 9, 1986.

Running Card: Every street box in the city has a running card assigned to it. There are over 2700 fire alarm boxes. Each card has a preplanned response assigned.

The first alarm assignment is described above under Box Alarm.

The second alarm gets four more engines, two ladders, the Deputy (if not on the first alarm), the rehab unit (W25), Safety Chief (H1), a second alarm chief, an Accountability chief (Net chief), and an evacuation chief if one is needed.

Third alarm: 2 engines, 1 ladder

Fourth alarm: 2 engines

Fifth alarm: 2 engines, 1 ladder

Sixth alarm: 2 engines

Seventh alarm: 2 engines, 1 ladder

Eighth alarm: 2 engines

Ninth alarm: 2 engines

Every box alarm has a RIT (Rapid Intervention Team) engine company assigned. Upon confirmation of a fire, a RIT ladder company and RIT district chief also respond.

Starting at the fifth alarm, the city receives Mutual Aid in the form of covering companies from the Metro Fire area.

Street Box: The City of Boston has fought vigorously over the years to retain the alarm boxes that have been on the street corners for over 300 years. These boxes know no language barrier, always work, and are the most reliable way to summon fire companies. When an alarm is received from a street box, one engine and one ladder company respond with a DFC.

Trucks: Ladder companies in the city have always been known as truck companies.

Lightning Source UK Ltd.
Milton Keynes UK
08 June 2010

155296UK00001B/162/P

9 781425 18068